How To ~~Pass~~ Blitz! ABRSM Theory
Grade 1

by Samantha Coates

Chester Music

Published by
Chester Music

Exclusive Distributors:
Hal Leonard
7777 West Bluemound Road,
Milwaukee, WI 53213
Email: info@halleonard.com

Hal Leonard Europe Limited
42 Wigmore Street Marylebone,
London, W1U 2 RY
Email: info@halleonardeurope.com

Hal Leonard Australia Pty. Ltd.
4 Lentara Court Cheltenham,
Victoria, 9132 Australia
Email: info@halleonard.com.au

Order No. CH87142
ISBN 978-1-78558-935-5
This book © Copyright 2017 Chester Music Limited

For all works contained herein:
Unauthorized copying, arranging, adapting, recording, Internet posting, public performance, or other distribution of the music in this publication is an infringement of copyright. Infringers are liable under the law.

Printed in EU.

www.halleonard.com

A Note From the Author

Dear theory student,

Congratulations! You have just done the very best thing for your music theory education — you've bought this book.

How To Blitz! ABRSM Theory Grade 1 contains more information, more revision and more worksheets than any other theory textbook.

One of the best features is the clearest and easiest section on music notation ever written. It assumes you've never actually seen music before. If you already know how to read music, you will find this section SUPER EASY!!! Whizz through it and impress all your friends.

Although music theory applies to all instruments, not just piano, it is the piano keyboard that is most helpful in demonstrating certain things you need to learn, such as semitones and accidentals. The reason for this is that the piano keyboard has a visual pattern. If you are learning to play an instrument other than piano, you'll find plenty of piano keyboard diagrams in the book to help you understand some of the concepts more easily.

So, have fun and enjoy working through this book. Every time you see this icon it means there are more practice examples you can download from the BlitzBooks website. Go to www.blitzbooks.com to download FREE manuscript, flashcards, worksheets and more!

Happy theory-ing,

Samantha

It takes more than an author and a publisher to produce a book — it takes enormous support from friends and family. Thank you to everyone who has helped me on the BlitzBooks journey, but most of all to Andrew, Thomas and Courtney... without you three, there would simply be no books.

Contents

A Little Bit About Rhythm 5

Introduction to Pitch Notation 6

Stems 12

More About Rhythm: Semiquavers 14

Dots and Ties 15

Time Signatures and Bar-lines 16

Drawing Rests Correctly 19

Quick Quiz 21

Leger Lines 22

Revision of Stuff So Far 23

Sharps, Flats and Naturals (a.k.a. 'Accidentals') 24

Tones, Semitones and The Major Scale 28

Scale-Degree Numbers 31

Tiny Test 33

Key Signatures vs Accidentals 34

Naming Notes in Melodies 36

More on Accidentals 37

Timed Test 38

Back to Rhythm: Adding Bar-lines 39

Grouping 40

Intervals 42

Rather Short Test 45

Tonic Triads 46

Word Search 49

Terms and Signs 50

Timed Test II 53

Copying Music 54

The Very Last Revision Test (promise) 56

Mad Multiple Choice 58

Test Paper... Sort Of 61

A Little Bit About Rhythm

This is just a tiny introduction to the different ways music notes are written. The shape of a note determines its length, or number of 'beats'. Lots more about this later on!

Note	Name	Number of Beats
o	semibreve	4
𝅗𝅥.	dotted minim	3
𝅗𝅥	minim	2
♩	crotchet	1
♪	quaver	$\frac{1}{2}$
♪ + ♪ = ♫	two quavers joined	$\frac{1}{2} + \frac{1}{2} = 1$
♪ + ♪ + ♪ + ♪ = ♬	four quavers joined	$\frac{1}{2} + \frac{1}{2} + \frac{1}{2} + \frac{1}{2} = 2$

In music there are also symbols to show lengths of silence. These are called RESTS.

Rest	Name	Number of Beats
𝄻	semibreve rest / whole bar rest	4 beats OR whole bar of silence
𝄼	minim rest	2
𝄽	crotchet rest	1
𝄾	quaver rest	$\frac{1}{2}$

Here is a rhythm quiz. Add up the beats!

1. 𝅗𝅥 + 𝅗𝅥. = ___
2. ♩ + 𝄾 = ___
3. ♬ + 𝅗𝅥 = ___
4. ♫ + 𝄽 = ___
5. ♩ + ♩ + ♬ = ___
6. o + ♩ = ___
7. ♫ + 𝅗𝅥. = ___
8. 𝄾 + 𝄼 + ♪ = ___

Introduction to Pitch Notation

As well as rhythm, music has pitch - sounds that are high, middle or low. Pitch is shown on sets of five lines, called a 'staff' or 'stave'. We'll refer to it both ways throughout this book. Here are some semibreves on a stave:

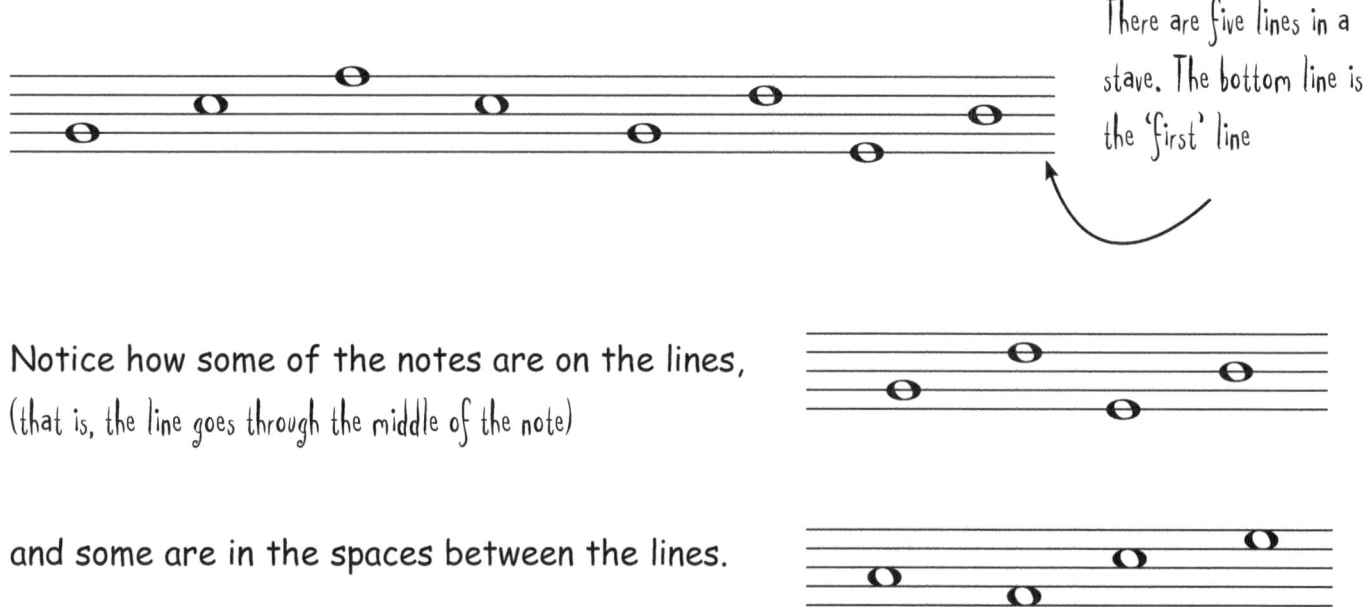

There are five lines in a stave. The bottom line is the 'first' line

Notice how some of the notes are on the lines, (that is, the line goes through the middle of the note)

and some are in the spaces between the lines.

Piano music is actually written on two staves bracketed together, called a 'grand stave':

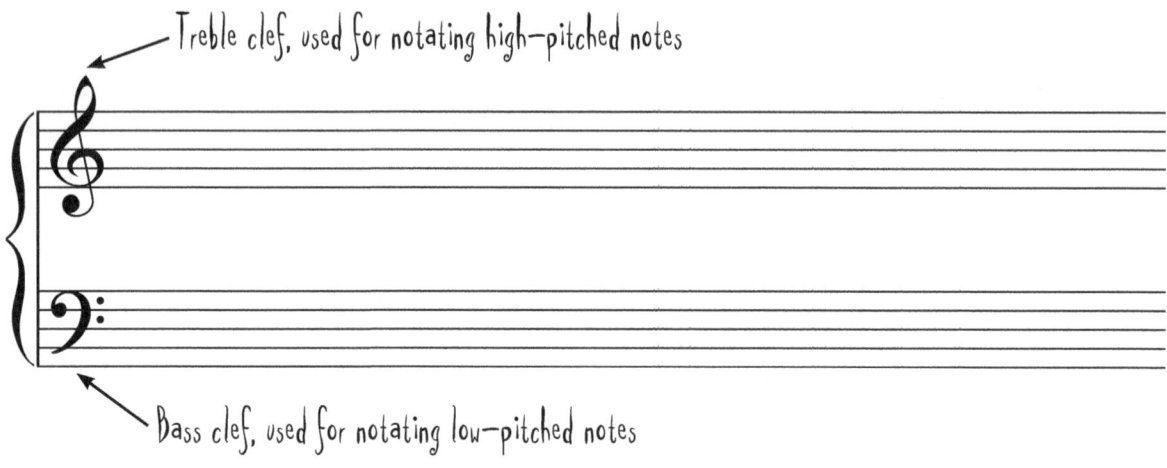

Treble clef, used for notating high-pitched notes

Bass clef, used for notating low-pitched notes

Draw some semibreves on the grand stave above. Put some in the treble, some in the bass, some on the lines and some in the spaces! (Oh dear that actually nearly rhymes)

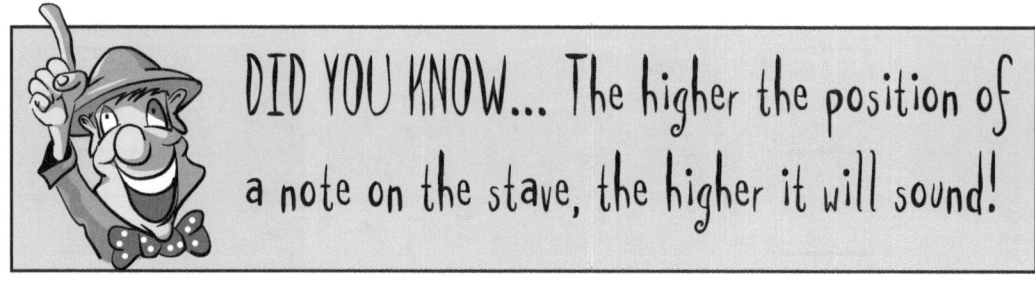

DID YOU KNOW... The higher the position of a note on the stave, the higher it will sound!

The Unofficial History of Middle C

Once upon a time, music used to be written on 11 lines, like this:

Middle C lives here

The note named 'C' lived on the line right in the middle. It was called 'Middle C'.

Many people found it very confusing looking at 11 lines all the time, and found it even more confusing trying to find Middle C. Then one day, somebody came up with the idea of taking out the middle line, leaving two sets of five lines.

Now the line for Middle C is invisible!

This was much easier to look at! Then look what happened:

The two sets of lines were moved even further apart; the top set was given a treble clef and the bottom set a bass clef, leaving space for Middle C in between. And so the grand stave was born!

Grand stave

It was decided that Middle C would need its own short line, called a 'leger line'. Middle C is always written close to either bass or treble, never floating in between.

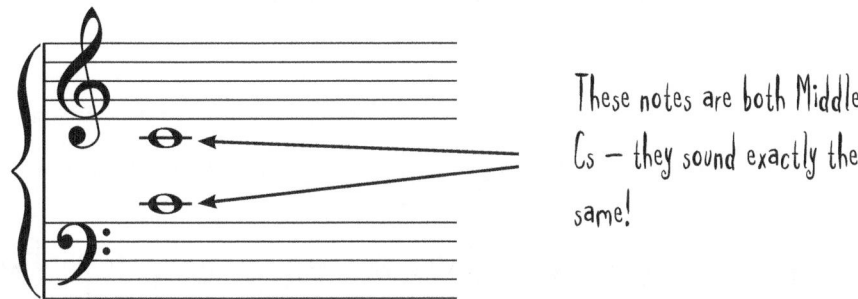

These notes are both Middle Cs — they sound exactly the same!

Some instruments, like the flute, are high pitched, which means they mostly play notes above Middle C. These instruments only need a treble clef to show their notes:

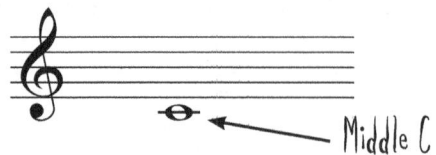

Other instruments, like the trombone, are low pitched, which means they mostly play notes below Middle C. These instruments need a bass clef to show their notes:

A piano has the largest range of notes of any musical instrument, so it needs a 'grand stave' to show them all. You will notice that the names of the notes are the same as the first seven letters of the alphabet, repeated over and over again:

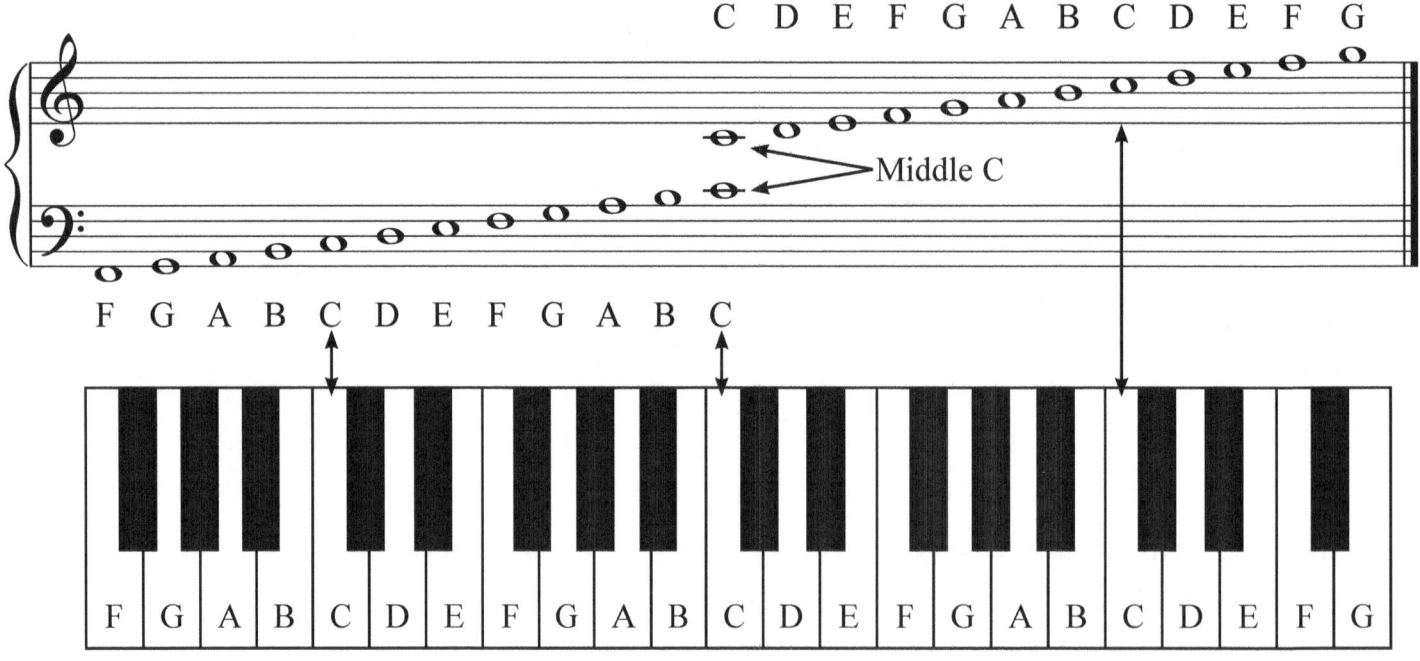

FACT: The piano keyboard has even more keys than this, but we've run out of room on the grand stave! Extremely high or extremely low notes are written using 'leger lines'. (See p.22)

Drawing Treble and Bass Clefs

The treble clef starts on the line where G lives, then winds around like this. Then it goes up and makes a loop above the staff and as it comes down it intersects on the fourth line. (Very important!)

Trace these treble clefs and then draw some of your own.

The bass clef starts on the line where F lives, then curls around like a backwards 'c', stopping just before the bottom line. Then two dots are added either side of the fourth line. (Also very important!)

Trace and draw some bass clefs here.

Here is a slightly smaller staff to write on. You'll need to get used to this size for your exam. Draw a whole load of treble and bass clefs!

HERE'S A THOUGHT... The treble clef used to be called the G clef and the bass clef used to be called the F clef. Can you figure out why?

Treble-Clef Notes

You can work out the names of all the notes in the treble from G. Fill in the rest!

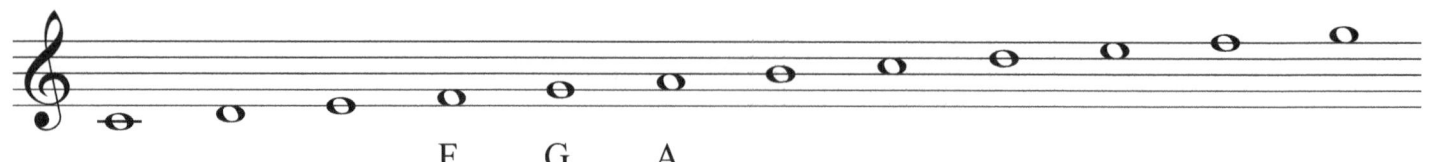

F　　G　　A

Quick Quiz:

How many are named F? ___ Which F is on a line, the lower F or the higher F? _____

Name four different notes that live in spaces. ___ ___ ___ ___

There are two notes named E, the lower E is on a _____, the higher E is in a _____.

There are two notes named D, the lower D is in a _____, the higher D is on a _____.

(P.S. If the note is sitting above or hanging below the stave, it's still 'in a space')

Can you name these notes? (Without peeking at the top of the page???)

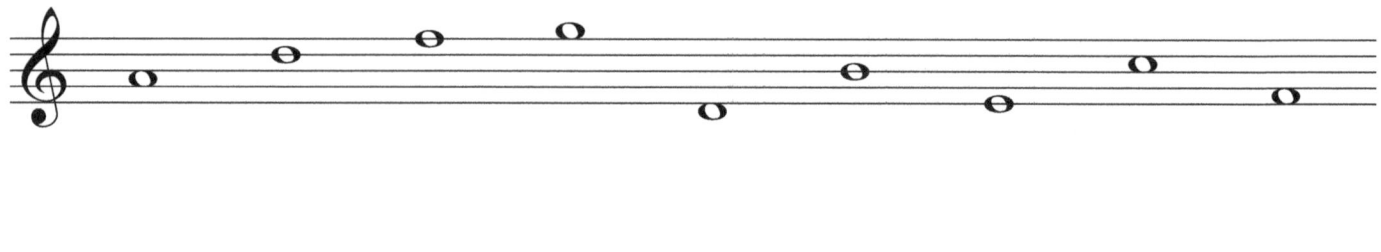

Draw a new treble clef in every bar below, and then write these notes!

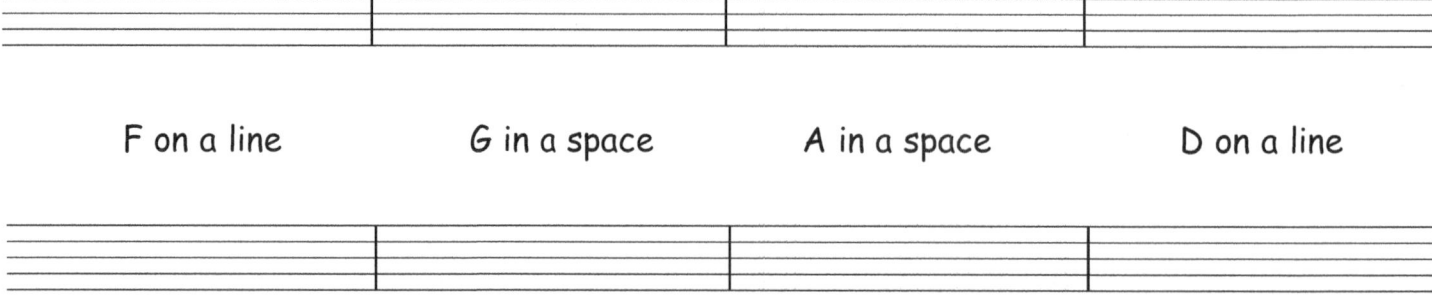

F on a line　　　　G in a space　　　　A in a space　　　　D on a line

G on a line　　　　C on a line　　　　E in a space　　　　D in a space

Bass-Clef Notes

You can also work out the names of the bass notes from F on the fourth line... fill these in!

                                          E   F   G

Now name these notes. (Remember that F lives on the fourth line — you can work out all the other notes from there!)

....

And now, draw a bass clef in each of these bars and write the following notes:

A in a space	D on a line	A on a line	C in a space

B in a space	F on a line	G on a line	E in a space

11

Stems

So far we've only been using semibreves (𝅝) to draw notes on staves. Now we're going to use other note values, which have stems (𝅗𝅥. 𝅗𝅥 ♩) and sometimes tails too (♪).

A stem can go up on the right side of the note (♩), or down on the left side (𝅘𝅥). The direction of the stem depends on where the note sits.

Notes BELOW the third line (which is the middle line) of the staff have their stems going **UP**.

The stems go on the right, like the letter 'd'.

Notes ABOVE the middle line of the staff have their stems going **DOWN**.

The stems go on the left, like the letter 'p'.

Notes sitting right **ON** the middle line can either go up or down – you can choose!

Remember 'd' for dogs and 'p' for puppies!

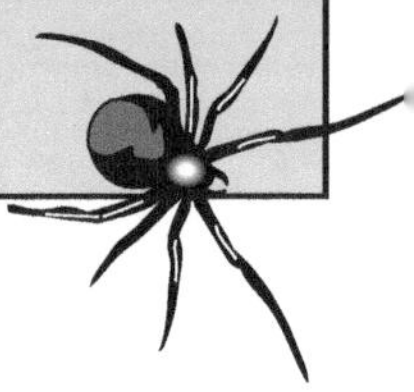

Handy Hint: Stems should be roughly the same height as the actual staff. To make sure your stems are the right height, draw them so they reach to the next note of the same letter name (also known as an 'octave above'), e.g.

is too short but

The next 'E' lives here

is just right!

1. Make these note heads into minims by adding stems in the correct direction. Remember 'd' for dogs and 'p' for puppies!

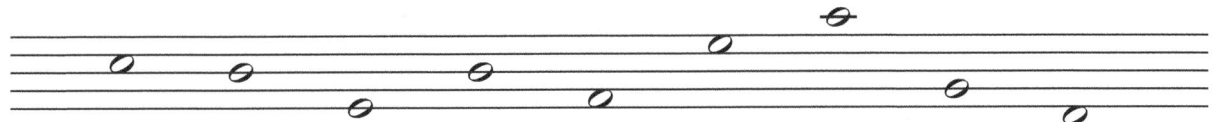

2. Now add a dot to each note to make all the minims above into dotted minims. (If the note is on a line, draw the dot in the space just above, otherwise we won't see it!)

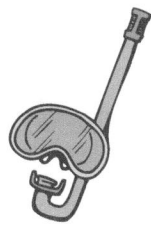

3. Make these note heads into crotchets. You'll need to colour them in AND add stems!

4. Make the following into quavers by adding a stem and a tail (♪ or ♪). The quaver tail always goes forwards (to the right) even if the stem is going down.

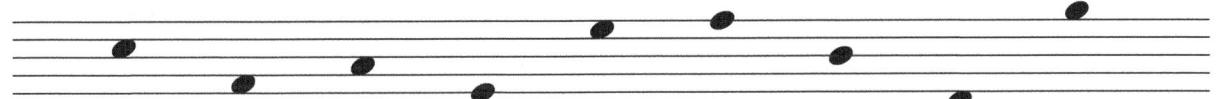

5. Two quavers can be joined together by a 'beam', e.g. ♫ or ♫ . Both stems MUST go in the same direction. In pairs where one stem would go up and the other down, e.g. , the note furthest from the middle line 'wins', like this: ! In fact, no matter how many notes are under the beam, majority rules!

Make these note heads into pairs of quavers. Draw the stems first, then add 'beams'.

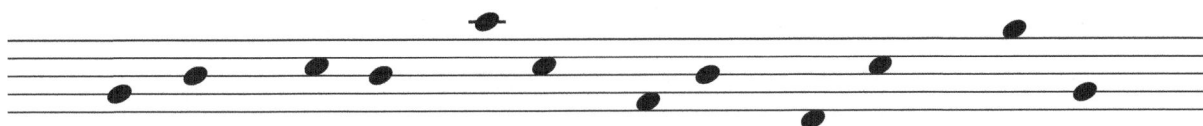

More about Rhythm: Semiquavers

Go back to page 5 and revise the rhythm values there. Then you'll be ready for this page!

Note	Name	Number of Crotchet Beats
♬	semiquaver	$\frac{1}{4}$
𝄿	semiquaver rest	$\frac{1}{4}$
♬ + ♬ = ♬♬	two semiquavers	$\frac{1}{4} + \frac{1}{4} = \frac{1}{2}$
♬ + ♬ + ♬ + ♬ = ♬♬♬♬	four semiquavers	$\frac{1}{4} + \frac{1}{4} + \frac{1}{4} + \frac{1}{4} = 1$

Semiquavers are almost always grouped four at a time. There are SIXTEEN semiquavers in one semibreve!

Sometimes you will see a mixture of quavers and semiquavers beamed (grouped) together. All of the following combinations are equivalent to one crotchet beat:

♪ + ♬ + ♬ = ♫♬   ♬ + ♬ + ♪ = ♬♫   ♬ + ♪ + ♬ = ♬♪♬

Quavers and semiquavers are beamed to show the crotchet beats wherever possible. All the stems must go in the same direction, and majority rules! (Revise your stem direction rules on the previous page)

So this  becomes this

How many crotchet beats are in each of these groups of quavers/semiquavers?

 ____    ____   ____    ____

Dots and Ties

A dot next to a note makes it longer. The dot equals half the value of the note.

That's why a dotted minim has three beats: 𝅗𝅥. is the same as 𝅗𝅥 + ♩ (2 + 1) (amazing, huh?).

So ♩. is the same as ♩ + ♪ = 1½ beats.

And ♪. is the same as ♪ + ♬ = ¾ of one beat.

Can you figure out the value of these dotted notes and rests?

(this is a super-hard one!)

𝄽. ____   𝄾. ____   𝅝. ____   𝄼. ____   ♪♪ ____

Important facts about dotted notes in Grade 1:

1. A dotted crotchet MUST be followed by a quaver e.g. ♩. ♪ (or something equivalent to a quaver!) This is because a note worth one-and-a-half beats must be made up to two beats.

2. A dotted quaver is ALWAYS followed by a semiquaver e.g. ♪.♬ (or something equivalent to a semiquaver!) This is because a note worth three-quarters of a beat must be made up to a whole beat.

A tie looks like this ⌣ and connects two notes of the same pitch.

For example: [notes tied] is a tie but [notes slurred] is a slur (meaning 'to play smoothly').

When two notes are tied, the second note is not played – the first note is held for the value of both notes.

So [tied notes] sounds exactly the same as [single note]!

These tied notes combine to make one sound. What is the value of each?

♩ ♩. 2½   𝅗𝅥 ♪. ____   𝅗𝅥 ♩. ____   ♩. ♩. ____

Time Signatures and Bar-lines

Time signatures and bar-lines are an extremely important part of music. Without them, it would be hard to play any sort of rhythm.

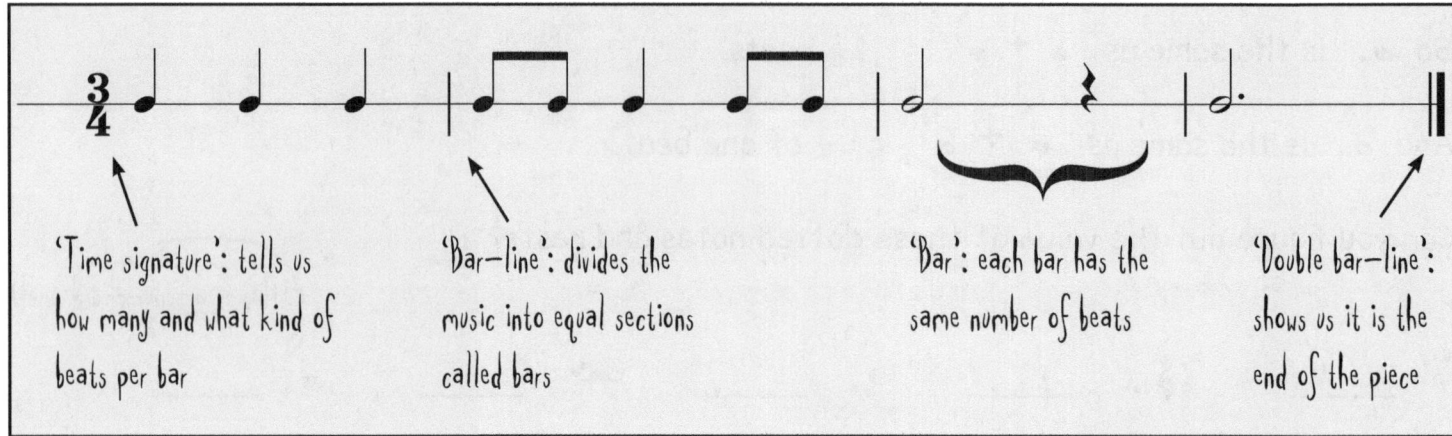

A time signature gives us information about the rhythm of a piece. There are always two numbers, one on top of the other. The top number tells us the **number** of beats, and the bottom number tells us what **kind** of beats.

The time signatures $\frac{2}{4}$, $\frac{3}{4}$ and $\frac{4}{4}$ all have a '4' on the bottom, meaning 'crotchet' beats.

$\frac{2}{4}$ means 'two crotchet beats per bar'. The formal name is 'simple duple'. Here's a rhythm in simple duple time. Count aloud two beats, then clap it:

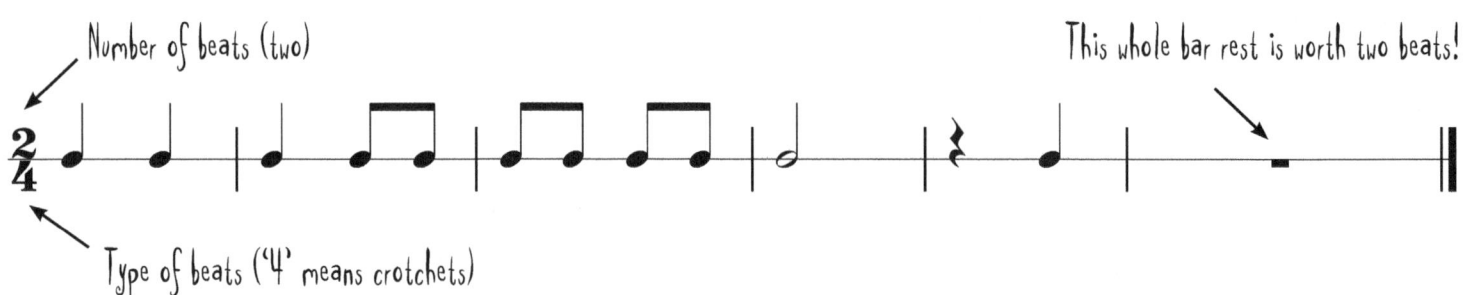

Here is a slightly more complicated version. Try clapping this one!

Count up the number of beats in each bar. Do they all have the same number of beats?

$\frac{3}{4}$ means 'three crotchet beats per bar'. The formal name is 'simple triple'. Try clapping this rhythm in simple triple time (count aloud to three first!):

In $\frac{3}{4}$, six quavers can all be grouped together under one beam

$\frac{4}{4}$ means 'four crotchet beats per bar'. The formal name is 'simple quadruple'. Now count in four beats then clap this rhythm:

Another very common time signature is this: **C**. That's right, it's the letter 'C', and it is known as 'common time'. **C** is exactly the same as $\frac{4}{4}$.

So **C** = common time = $\frac{4}{4}$ = four crotchet beats per bar = simple quadruple! (phew!)

Here's another rhythm to clap, in common time (simple quadruple):

★ Count up the beats in each bar. There should be 4!

And now for a challenge... can you figure out the time signature of these rhythms? Practise clapping them with your teacher – it's a really important skill to be able to clap rhythms!

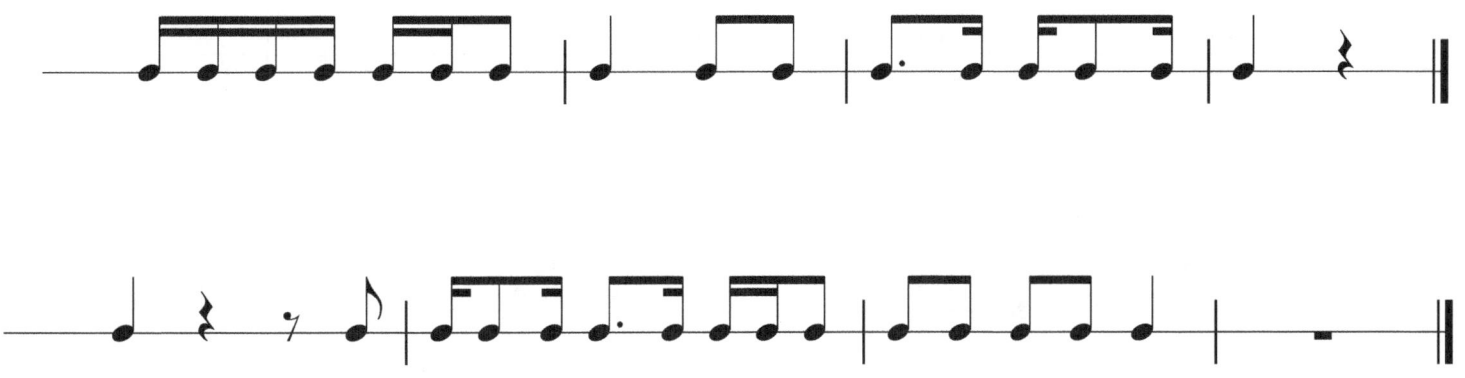

Adding Time Signatures

This is sooooo easy. You will only be tested on the time signatures $\frac{2}{4}$, $\frac{3}{4}$, and $\frac{4}{4}$. All you have to do is count up the number of beats in each bar, and then write the time signature at the beginning. (You may remember you just did this at the end of the previous page!)

When you write time signatures, the top and bottom numbers should each take up two spaces within the stave, like this $\frac{2}{4}$ not like this $\frac{2}{4}$!

Add the correct time signature to these six melodies.

← These symbols are called key signatures! See page 29

Drawing Rests Correctly

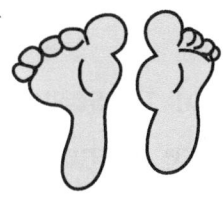

Crotchet Rests

Think of the crotchet rest as starting off a bit like the letter 'Z'  with the letter 'C' springing off the bottom. It must start in the top space and finish in the bottom space. Trace and draw some crotchet rests on this staff:

Minim Rests

Minim rests sit on the **third** line of the staff. They must not take up the whole space between the lines; draw them like this not like this !

Trace and draw some minim rests:

Whole Bar Rests (Semibreve Rests)

These hang from the fourth line and, like minim rests, must not take up the whole space! Trace and draw some here:

Quaver and Semiquaver Rests

A quaver rest is sort of like a curvy number '7'. A semiquaver rest is similar, but with an extra hook. They both sit inside the middle two spaces. Trace and draw some here:

Complete These Bars

Each of these melodies have some missing rests. Every time you see an asterisk, your job is to write in the correct rest to complete the bar. All you have to do is COUNT up the beats and figure out how many are missing... and watch out for the changing time signatures!

In these melodies, there are missing rests AND a missing time signature!

Quick Quiz

1. Add the correct time signature to these melodies.

2. Draw the clef to make these notes correct.

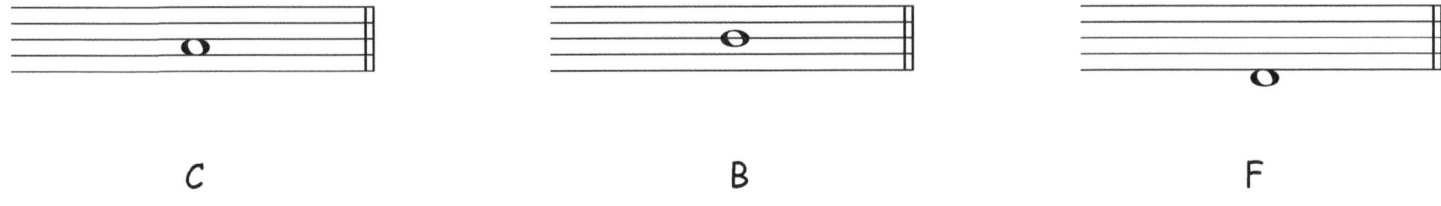

       C   B   F

4. Draw Middle C here:

5. Write the rests that have the equivalent value to these notes:

6. Write the correct rest at each place marked with an asterisk (*).

21

Leger Lines

Leger lines are miniature staff lines used to show very high or very low notes. In Grade 1 we're only tested on one leger line above or below the stave, but there's actually no limit to how many you can use in general music!

Wow! What note is THAT???

Here are some treble notes on leger lines. Copy them in the spaces provided.

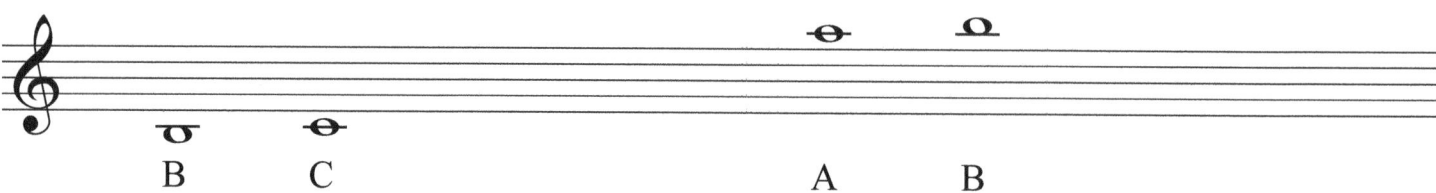

B   C   A   B

And now here are some bass notes on leger lines! Once again, copy them.

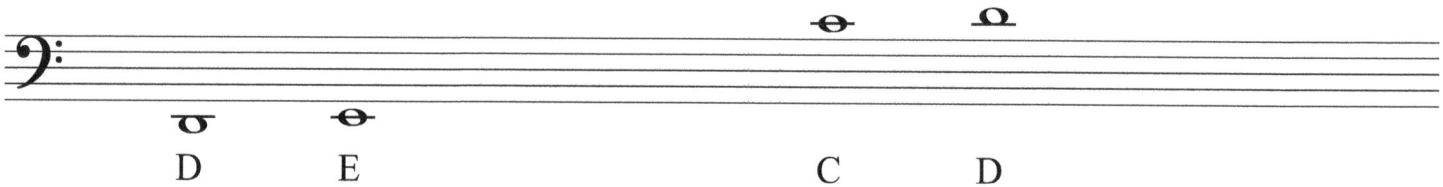

D   E   C   D

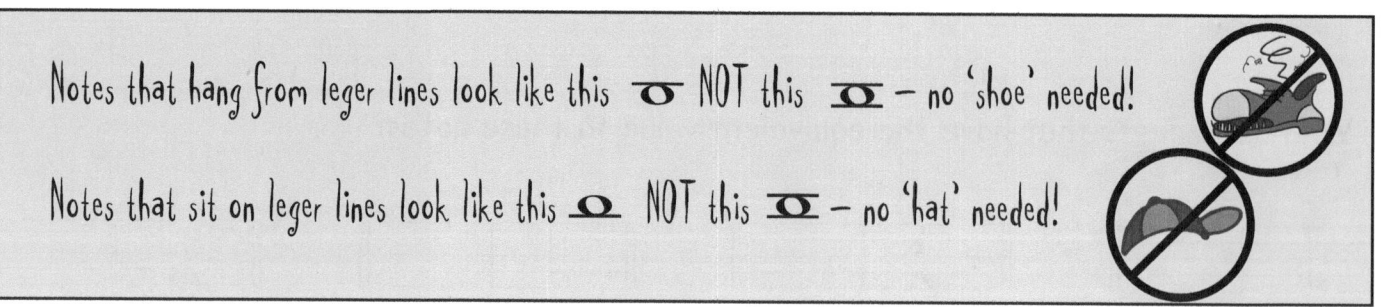

When drawing leger lines, keep them spaced the same distance apart as the staff lines. Draw the line first, then draw the note! Have fun drawing some here:

Revision of Stuff So Far

1. Name these notes. Watch out for clef changes!

    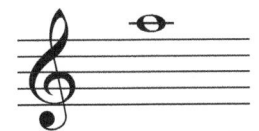 

   _____ _____ _____

2. Which notes sound higher in pitch, treble notes or bass notes? _____

3. ♩ + ♫ + 𝄻 + ♩. + 𝄽 + 𝅝 + ♪ = _____ beats

4. Draw these notes and clefs (you'll need to use leger lines for some!):

   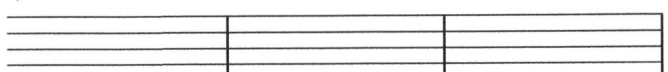   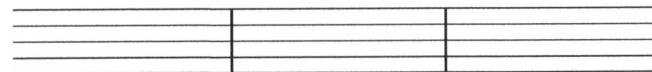

   B in three places in the treble   D in three places in the bass

5. Rewrite this melody, grouping/beaming the notes correctly.

   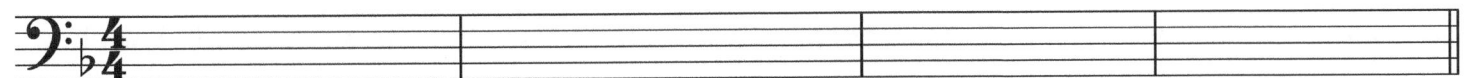

6. True or false: this note is named B.   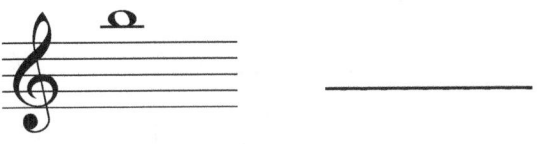 _____

23

Sharps, Flats and Naturals (a.k.a. 'Accidentals')

Sharp (♯), flat (♭) and natural (♮) signs are known as 'accidentals'. They are used to change the pitch of a note. Each of these signs will change the pitch by one 'semitone'.
A semitone is the distance between a note and its nearest neighbour.

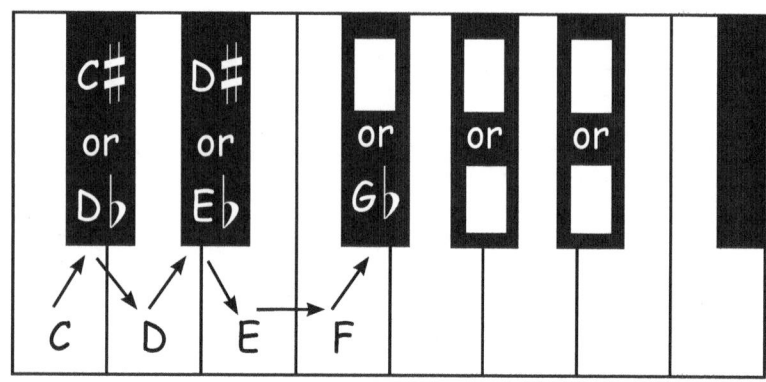

On a piano keyboard, the semitones are very easy to see. The arrows show the steps by semitones. C to C♯ is a semitone. E to F is also a semitone. See if you can fill in the rest of the names and arrows!

An accidental before a note will change the way it sounds:

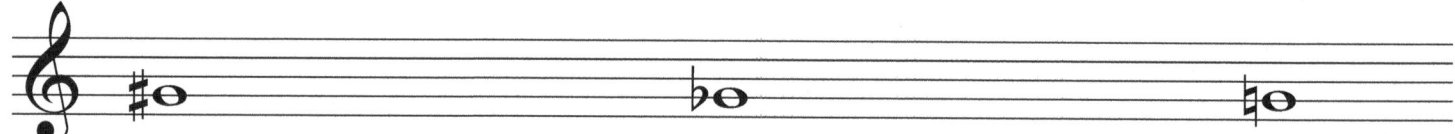

G sharp sounds one semitone higher than G.

G flat sounds one semitone lower than G.

G natural is the same as G – a natural sign cancels out a sharp or flat sign.

 DID YOU KNOW... Accidentals are always written BEFORE the note? So even though we say 'G-sharp', on the stave we write 'sharp-G'!

Play some notes with accidentals on your instrument. Notice how D♯ sounds the same as E♭, G♯ sounds the same as A♭, etc. Don't forget to try E♯ - it sounds the same as F! How about B♯? And what about C♭? Notes have more than one name... just like you do! Two notes with different names but the same sound are called 'enharmonic equivalents'.

Quick Quiz:
♯ = _____ sign = note sounds one semitone _____
♭ = _____ sign = note sounds one semitone _____
♮ = _____ sign = cancels out a _____ or a _____ sign

Sharps, flats and naturals can be tricky to draw. They must sit on exactly the same line or in exactly the same space as the note, and must also be just the right size.

Right	Wrong	Right	Wrong	Right	Wrong
♯o	♯ o	♭o	♭o	♮o	♮o

Sharps

Sharps look like a 'noughts and crosses' grid with the lines across sloping up.

Notice how the vertical lines are quite long. The 'middle square' is the part that must line up with the note. (See above)

Trace and draw some sharps next to these notes. (Remember, accidentals always go on the LEFT of the note)

Flats

Flats look like a lower case 'b' that is pointy at the bottom.

The round part of the flat must line up with the note. (See above)

Trace and draw some flats here:

 Go to **www.blitzbooks.com** and download some FREE manuscript to practise drawing notes with sharps and flats!

Naturals

These are the trickiest to draw. Imagine drawing an upper case 'L' 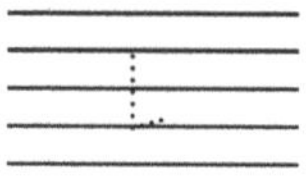  followed by another one upside down. The lines across slope up just a little bit! It must form a 'square' wherever the note is sitting (see previous page).

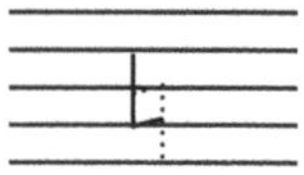

Trace and draw some natural signs here:

Add the correct accidental to these notes. (Remember, the sign goes BEFORE the note!)

F sharp   E natural   D flat   G sharp

F flat   D sharp   A natural   A flat

G flat   B sharp   G natural   C natural

Know Your Notes!

1. Write the following notes as semibreves:

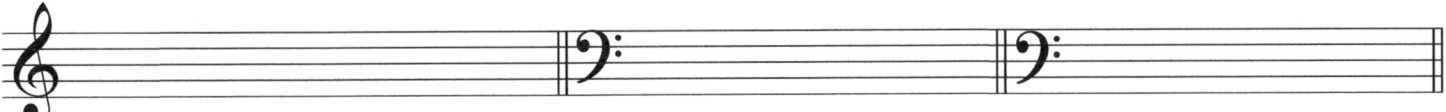

      E flat on a line   E below the staff   C sharp above the staff

2. Draw the following:

  B flat as a minim in the bass clef   D sharp as a quaver in the treble clef

3. Name these notes. Use words for ♯, ♭ and ♮. Watch out for clef changes!

....

4. Place the correct clef in each bar below, to make the note names correct:

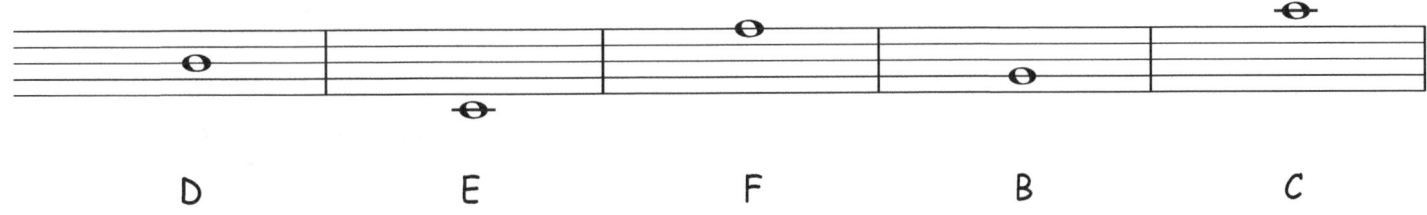

    D   E   F   B   C

5. Add a sign to this note to make it sound one semitone higher:

6. Now find your raised note from question 5 on the keyboard diagram on page 24.

   It's a black note... what is its 'enharmonic equivalent' (as in, what is another name for it)? _____

Tones, Semitones and the Major Scale

★ A 'semitone' is the distance between a note and its nearest neighbour. (See page 24)

★ A 'tone' is made up of two semitones – just like a circle is made up of two semicircles!

You've probably played some major scales before. They sound similar to each other, they just start on different notes. Major scales sound similar because they are all based on the following pattern:

Tone-Tone-Semitone-Tone-Tone-Tone-Semitone (T-T-S-T-T-T-S)

Let's look at the C major scale:

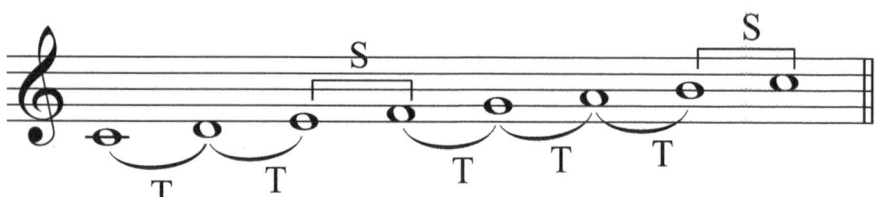 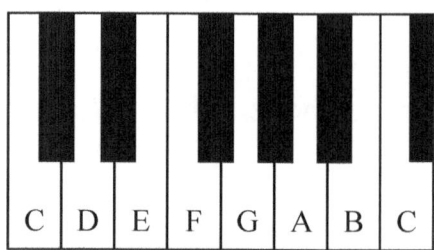

> It just so happens that C major does not need any sharps or flats to make the right pattern. This is why **C major has NO SHARPS OR FLATS**.

How about G major:

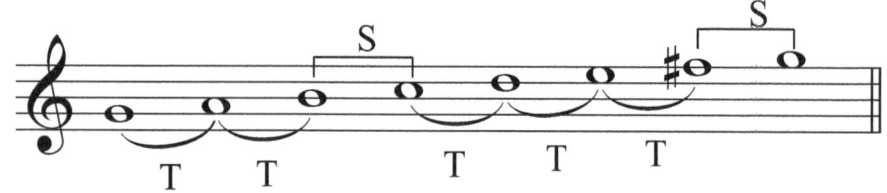 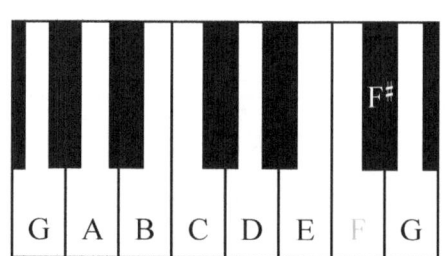

> E to F is only a semitone. We need the F♯ to make a tone in the right spot.
> This is why **G major has an F SHARP**.

Now for the F major scale:

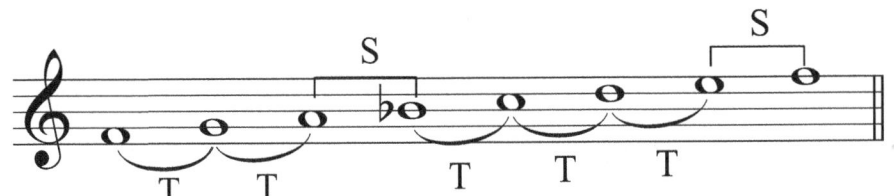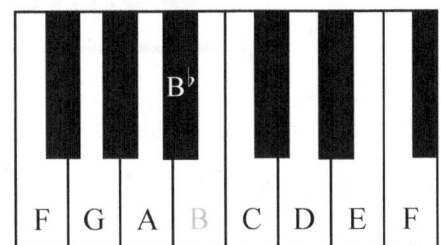

> A to B is a tone, so we need the B♭ to make a semitone in the right spot.
> This is why **F major has a B FLAT**.

And finally, the D major scale:

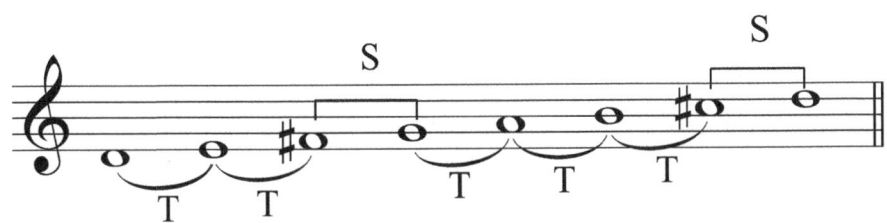

> The F and C must be raised, otherwise the pattern will not be correct.
> This is why **D major has F SHARP and C SHARP**.

If you know which sharps or flats are in a scale, then you know its **KEY SIGNATURE**. A key signature shows what scale a piece of music is based on.

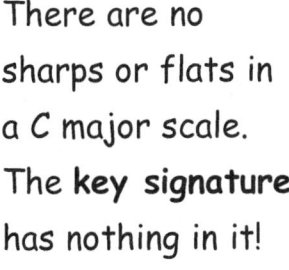

There are no sharps or flats in a C major scale. The **key signature** has nothing in it!

There is an F sharp in the scale of G major, so the **key signature** of G major is F♯.

There is a B flat in the scale of F major, so the **key signature** of F major is B♭.

The scale of D major contains F♯ and C♯, so the **key signature** of D major is F♯ and C♯.

Semitones in Major Scales

Sometimes you are asked to 'mark the semitones' in a scale. This usually means you'll need to put a square bracket like this ⌐‾‾⌐ over the notes that are a semitone apart.

Turn back one page and notice how the scales are marked in tones and semitones. All you need to remember is (going from lowest to highest) **T-T-S, T-T-T-S** (say this out loud 27 times).

Draw square brackets over the semitones in this D major scale:

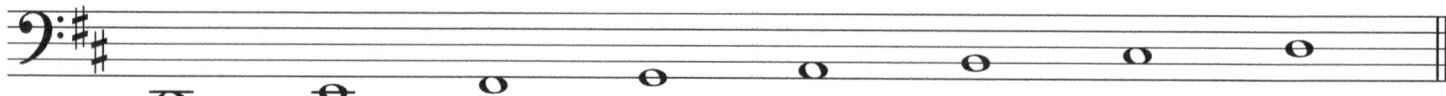

Good job! Now let's do it with a scale that's going down. Starting from the LOWEST note, work out where the semitones are and mark them with square brackets.

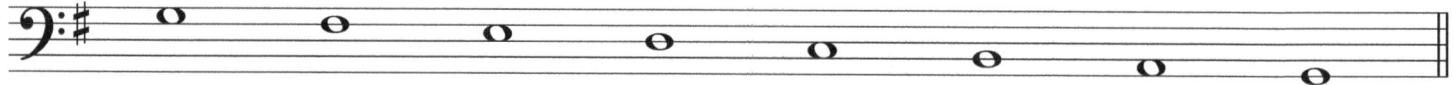

Just by the way, what scale is this?_____

Here are some scales written in interesting rhythms. Mark the semitones!

Scale Degree Numbers

Each note in the scale has a number. The **lowest** note is always the '1st' scale degree.

Finish writing the scale degree numbers under this D major scale.

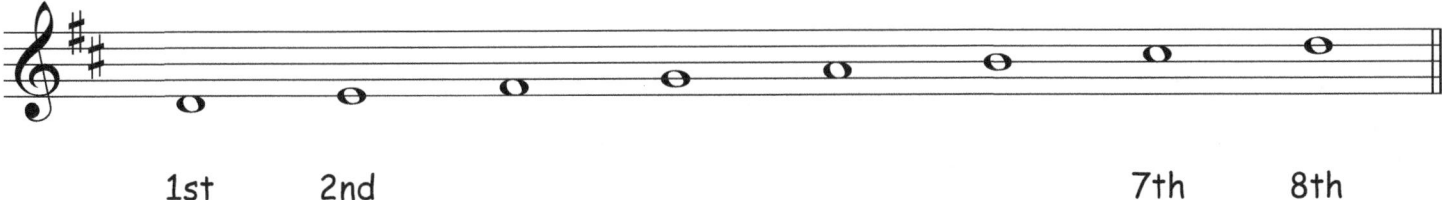

1st   2nd   7th   8th

Here's an F major scale that's going DOWN. Finish writing in the scale-degree numbers.

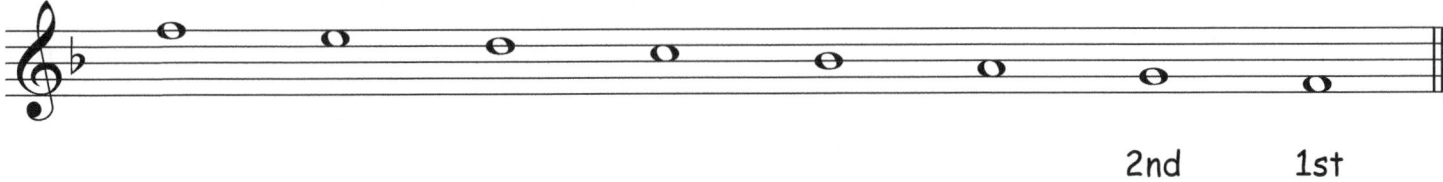

                                                                       2nd   1st

Mark the semitones in each of the scales above. What do you notice?

> **HOT TIP:** Semitones in major scales ALWAYS occur between scale degrees 3-4 and 7-8. You may find this easier to remember than TTSTTTS... whatever works for you!

Here is a G major scale all out of order. Write the scale degrees underneath the notes. (Remember, in your exam you have to write 1st, 2nd, 3rd etc. instead of 1, 2, 3):

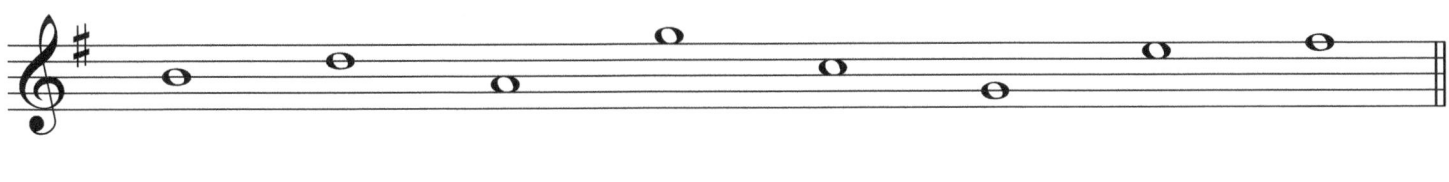

___   ___   ___   ___   ___   ___   ___   ___

Quick revision:

What is the name of scale degree no. 1 in C major? ___
What is the name of scale degree no. 1 in F major? ___
What is the name of scale degree no. 1 in G major? ___
What is the name of scale degree no. 1 in D major? ___

Do you notice a bit of a pattern here???

Scale Degrees in Melodies (that rhymes!)

Writing scale degrees under a melody is just like writing them under a scale, except that the notes are 'out of order'. A tune can start on any degree of the scale.

Write in the missing scale degrees for this famous tune in G major:

5th 1st 7th   1st   1st

 DID YOU NOTICE... the top G is labelled '1st', not '8th'? Every G is the 1st scale degree, every A is the 2nd, and so on. Although we used '8th' when we discussed the major scale, in melodies we only ever use 1st – 7th.

In your exam you are told the key and the first answer is usually given to you. All you need to do is count carefully, and the rest is easy!

Write the correct scale degree at each place marked with an asterisk in these melodies.

This one is in G major:

3rd   ....

And this one is in C major:

1st   ....

Terrific Work!

# Tiny Test

Total: /25

1. Mark each of these pairs of notes with an 'S' for semitone or a 'T' for tone.
   Use the diagram on page 24 to help you! /5

2. Here is a melody in D major. Label the scale-degree number at each asterisk. /8

7th.   ....

3. Write the following key signatures (watch out for the clef changes): /4

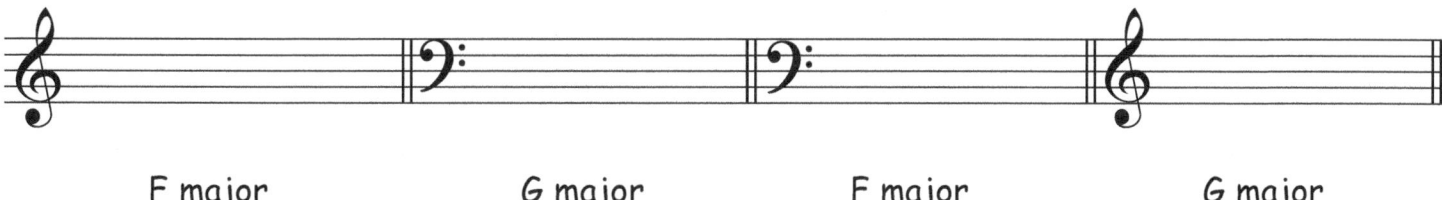

F major   G major   F major   G major

4. Add the correct key signature to this F major scale. Then mark the semitones. /2

5. Write the correct notes for these F major scale-degree numbers.
   Check the clef. (Warning: an accidental is required for one of the notes!) /6

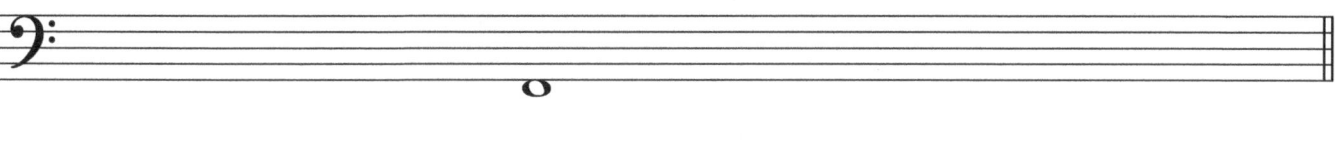

6th   4th   1st   5th   7th   3rd   2nd

33

Key Signatures vs Accidentals

Scales can be written two ways:

1. With the key signature at the beginning

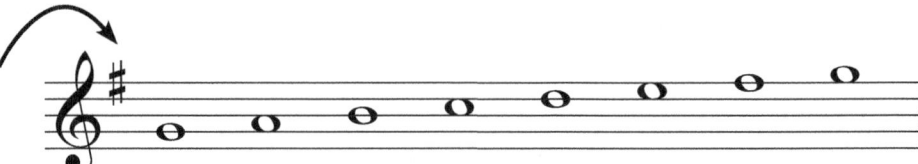

OR...

2. With an accidental instead of the key signature.

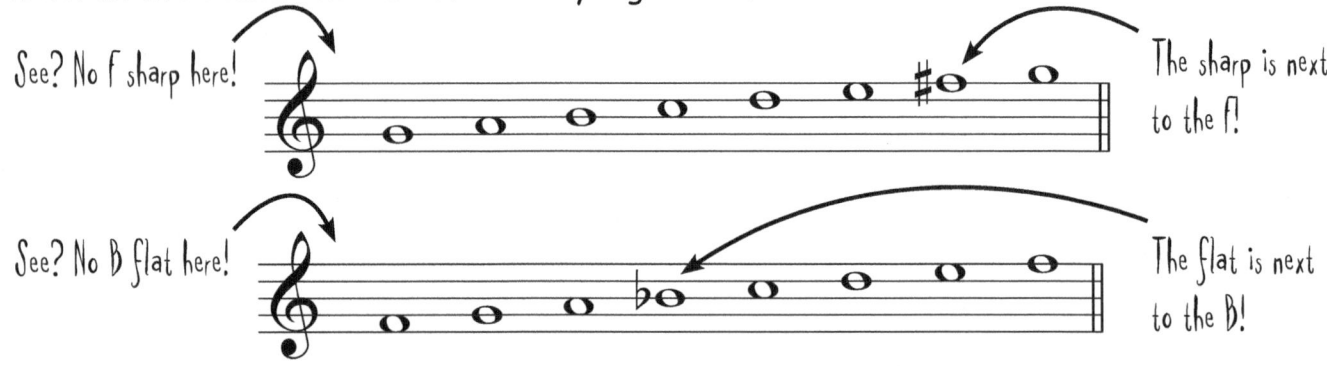

HOT TIP: Scales are written EITHER with a key signature at the beginning OR with an accidental in the right place — never both!

Write a G major scale here using semibreves. Write one octave ascending (going up), and use **accidentals** instead of a key signature.

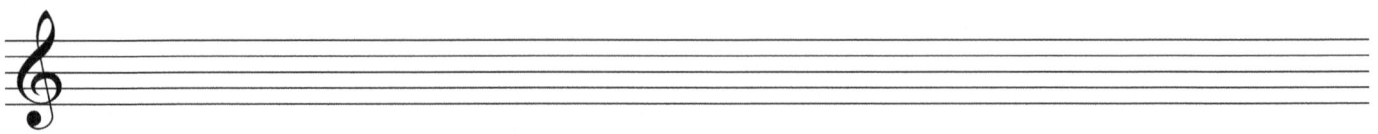

Now write an F major scale descending (going down), using crotchets. Write the key signature.

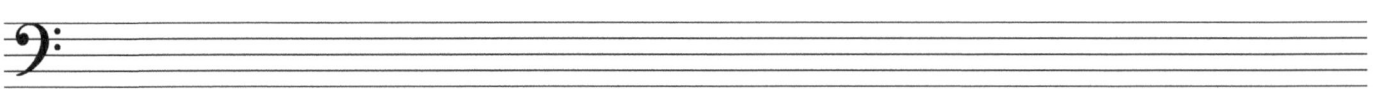

Tricky one now... add the correct **clef** and **accidentals** to make this a D major scale. (Ooaaahh)

Scale Practice (what joy)

1. Add the correct clef and accidentals to make this the scale of G major:

2. Now make the notes in the scale above into minims and mark the semitones with square brackets.

3. Write the scale of C major:

   ★ use accidentals (hint: this is a trick)
   ★ use crotchets
   ★ write one octave ascending
   ★ complete the scale with a double bar-line

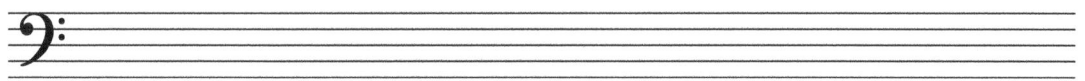

 Did you see the clef?

4. Name these scales:

Scale: _____

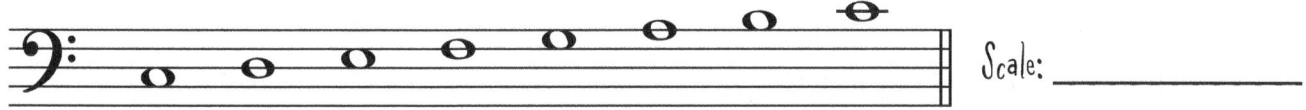

Scale: _____

Naming Notes in Melodies

It's time to use your note-naming skills with melodies. Not only do you have to write the letter name of the notes, you ALSO have to check the key signature... because your letter name might need a sharp or flat sign!

This note is not just C! It is C#, because of the key signature

At each place marked with * write the correct letter name underneath. Remember to check the key signature, and include any necessary sharp or flat signs in your answers. One of the answers is done for you in the first example (isn't that nice?!?).

 HERE'S A THOUGHT... it's pretty easy to practise this skill a lot. Just name any of the notes of your pieces!

More on Accidentals

As you learned on page 24, accidentals are used to change the pitch of a note.

★ The sharp sign (♯) makes a note one semitone _____

★ The flat sign (♭) makes a note one semitone _____

★ The natural sign (♮) makes a note one semitone _____ OR _____ !

Naturals cancel out sharps and flats. If you see a natural, you have to check which sign was **previously** on that note to know whether the natural is making the note higher or lower.

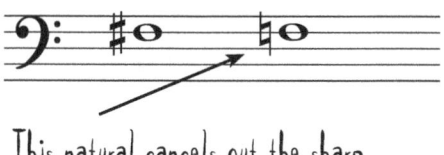

This natural cancels out the sharp, which makes the second note lower

This natural is cancelling out the flat, which makes the second note HIGHER

Circle the **higher** note of these pairs of notes. If the natural is on the first note of the pair, the answer is obvious. If the natural is on the second note of the pair, take care!

In this next set, circle the **lower** note of each pair. There are two which are rather obvious, but the last one is super tricky!!

If a natural suddenly appears in a melody, it is cancelling out the sharp or flat from the key signature.

Is this note higher or lower than the note before it? Check the key signature to find your answer!

Timed Test

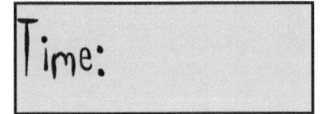

Time yourself doing this quiz. Do it as fast as you can, then record your finishing time above. But... guess what? Your teacher will **ADD ON 10 SECONDS** for every mistake you make! It's fun to go fast, but more important to be **accurate**. Start the clock!

1. How many quavers are there in this note? 𝅗𝅥. _____

2. Name this key signature:  _____

3. Which major scale contains one flat? _____

4. Finish this ascending major scale using minims. Then add the correct accidental!

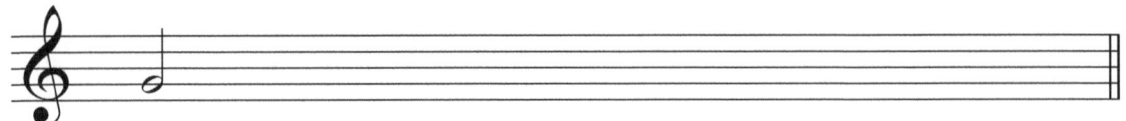

5. Using square brackets, mark the semitones in the scale above.

6. Circle the lower note in this pair:

7. Add the correct clef, key signature, time signature and missing bar-lines to this melody in F major.

STOP THE CLOCK - FILL IN YOUR TIME AT THE TOP!

After marking this with your teacher, tick one of the following:

☐ I made no mistakes! I keep my time of _____ !

☐ I made _____ mistakes. My new time is _____

Back to Rhythm: Adding Bar-lines

To add bar-lines to a melody, all you need to do is check the time signature and COUNT! Also, the first bar-line is usually put in for you, making it super easy.

Just a couple of handy tips:

★ Don't let ties and slurs put you off – bar-lines can cut through them.

★ Bar-lines CANNOT cut through groups of quavers!

★ If there is no double bar-line at the end, you'll need to add one yourself.

1. Add the missing bar-lines to these melodies (the first bar-line is given):

2. In these melodies you'll need to write the time signatures AND some bar-lines... tricky!

Grouping

Quavers are often grouped two at a time, to show the crotchet beats, e.g. ♪♪. In $\frac{2}{4}$ and $\frac{3}{4}$, bars of quavers are grouped together, like this $\frac{2}{4}$ ♫♫ or this $\frac{3}{4}$ ♫♫♫

In $\frac{4}{4}$, quavers are usually grouped four at a time, except...

NEVER GROUP FOUR QUAVERS ON BEATS 2 AND 3!

For instance, $\frac{4}{4}$ ♩♫♫♩ would be incorrect. It would have to be rewritten like this: $\frac{4}{4}$ ♩♫♫♩ so that the four quavers do not cross the middle of the bar.

Fill these bars with quavers correctly grouped:

$\frac{3}{4}$ _____ $\frac{4}{4}$ _____

There is a similar rule for the minim rest (𝄼):

NEVER PUT A MINIM REST ON BEATS 2 AND 3!

So $\frac{4}{4}$ ♩ 𝄼 ♩ is wrong. It would have to be rewritten like this $\frac{4}{4}$ ♩ 𝄽 𝄽 ♩

Don't use minim rests AT ALL in $\frac{3}{4}$ – always use crotchet rests! (P.S. You won't be tested on the grouping of rests in your Grade 1 exam, but it's good to know this stuff!)

Complete each of these bars as directed, with correct grouping of notes and rests.

$\frac{3}{4}$ | _____ | _____ | _____ | _____ |

       6 notes   1 note and 2 rests   1 rest   4 notes and 1 rest

HOT TIP: Grouping is a bit like spelling. Words can be spelled differently even though they sound the same. You must 'spell' your rhythms correctly!

The words 'grouping' and 'beaming' both mean pretty much the same thing. In the exam you are often asked to rewrite notes correctly grouped or beamed. We did a little of this back on page 14, but here are some slightly more complicated exercises (lucky you!).

One really important thing to know: ♪. ♪ when beamed together becomes ♪.♪ !

Rewrite these melodies making sure all the notes have correct beaming/grouping.

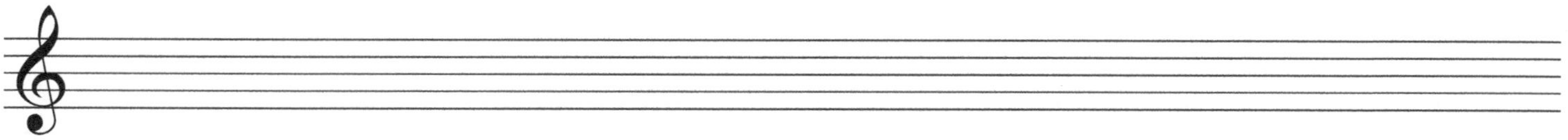

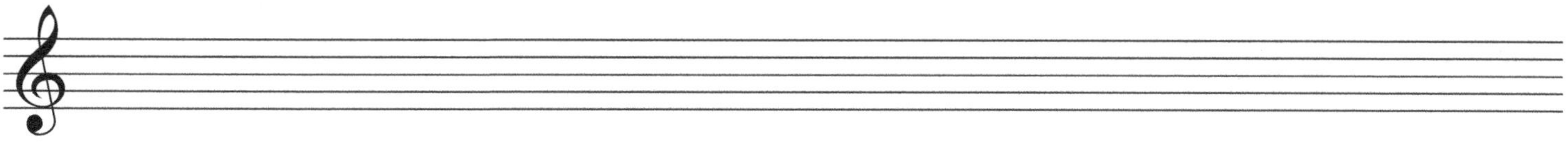

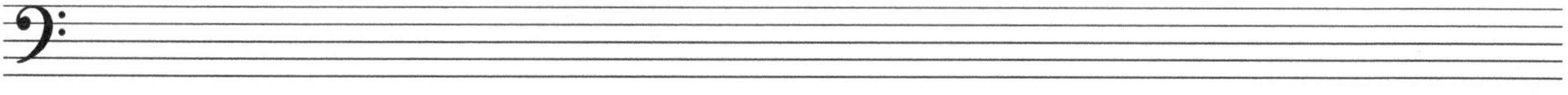

And now here is an extra challenge.. try fixing this melody, which has really awful grouping!

Intervals

★ An interval is the distance between two notes.

★ The bottom note is known as the 'tonic' note (i.e. scale degree no. 1).

★ An interval where both notes are the same pitch is called a 'unison' (it is never called a '1st').

There are two types of intervals: 'harmonic' and 'melodic'.

Harmonic intervals line up vertically (except for unisons and 2nds – see below) and sound together (like 'harmony'):

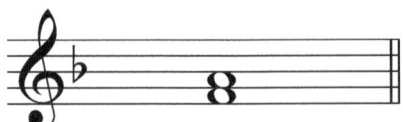

Melodic intervals are written side by side, and the notes sound separately, like a melody:

To name an interval, simply count up from the bottom note. Here are some harmonic intervals in C major (you can fill in the missing names):

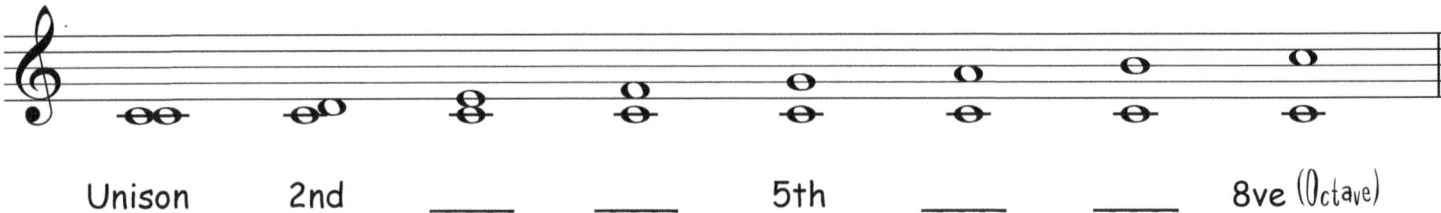

Unison   2nd   ____   ____   5th   ____   ____   8ve (Octave)

Name these melodic intervals above the tonic of F. (Hint: they are not in order!)

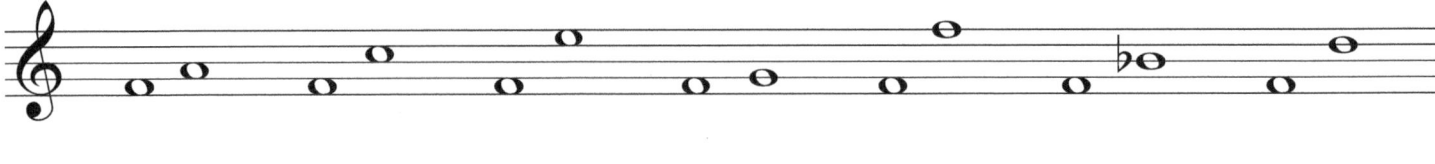

____   ____   ____   ____   ____   ____   ____

Name these harmonic intervals. The accidentals don't change the number... they are there because the higher note of the intervals comes from the SCALE of the lower tonic note.

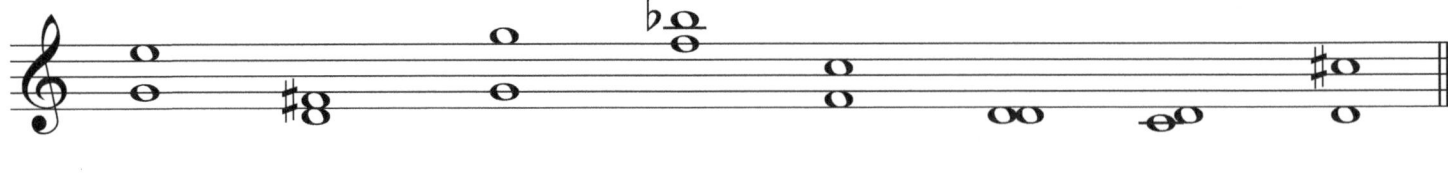

____   ____   ____   ____   ____   ____   ____

Writing Intervals is Easy

You will be asked to write either harmonic intervals OR melodic intervals. Always read the question carefully! One quick tip before you start: make sure your harmonic '2nd' is to the side like this ![], not squished above like this ![]!

1. Write these harmonic intervals (i.e. top note is directly above bottom note) above C.
   (OK, the unison won't be 'above'! It should be so close that it touches the tonic.)

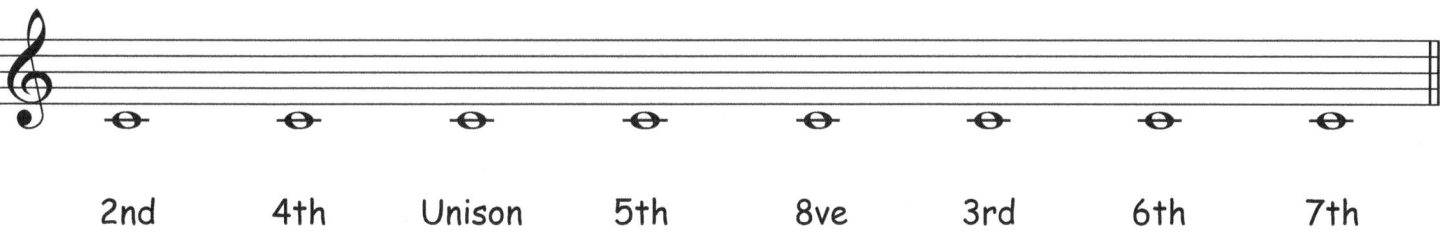

   2nd   4th   Unison   5th   8ve   3rd   6th   7th

2. Write these melodic intervals in D major. The first one is done for you.

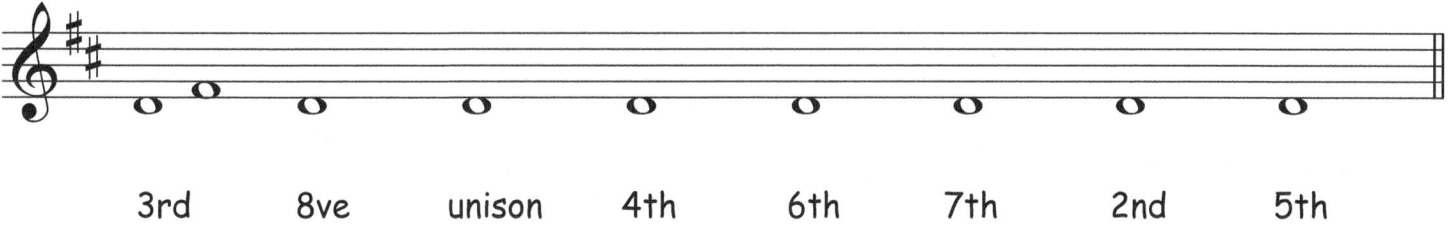

   3rd   8ve   unison   4th   6th   7th   2nd   5th

3. Write these key signatures and the named interval.

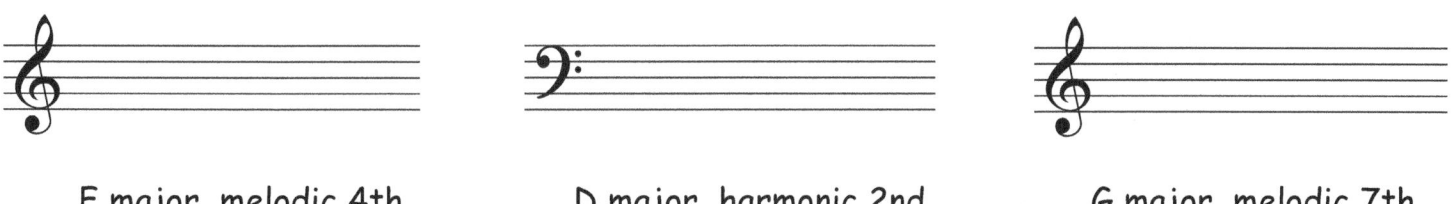

   F major, melodic 4th   D major, harmonic 2nd   G major, melodic 7th

Go to www.blitzbooks.com and download FREE worksheets on how to draw intervals with accidentals!

43

More Intervals

1. Name these harmonic intervals. They are all in F major.

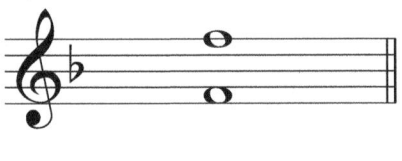 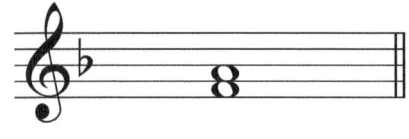 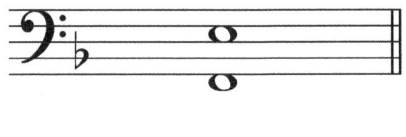

_____   _____   _____

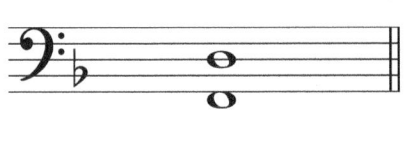 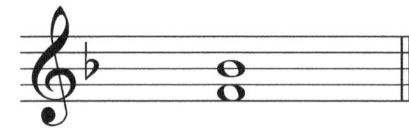 

_____   _____   _____

2. And now, name these melodic intervals. Which key are they in? _____

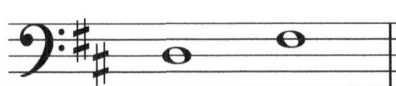 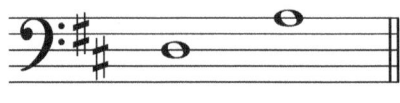 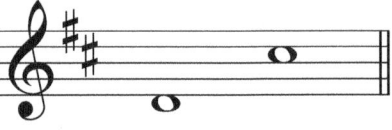

_____   _____   _____

_____   _____   _____

3. Intervals are always written **above** the tonic, even if you have to use leger lines. Write these harmonic intervals above the given tonic note:

5th   7th   7th   4th   3rd

4. What is an interval of an 8th usually called? _____

Rather Short Test

All of the questions in this test relate to this melody! Have fun...

1. The time signature of the melody above is 'C'. Which other time signature is this equivalent to? _____

2. In what key is the melody? _____

3. Find and circle all the '5th' scale degrees in the melody.

4. Rewrite it here, with correct grouping/beaming.

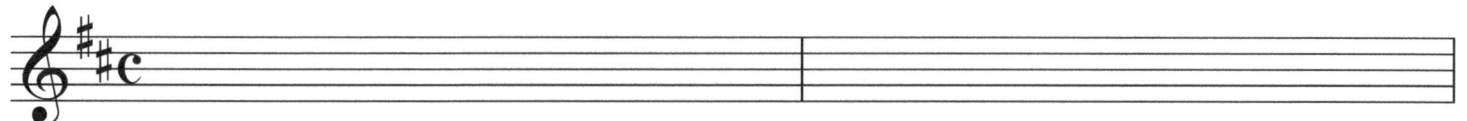

5. True or false: In bar 1 there are no intervals larger than a 3rd. _____

6. Using accidentals, write the scale that is in the same key as the melody above. Write one octave descending, using crotchets.

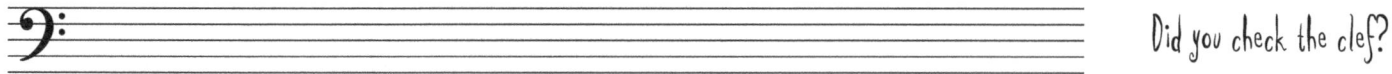

Did you check the clef?

45

Tonic Triads

* A 'chord' is two or more notes sounding together.

* A 'triad' is a chord made up of three notes.

* A 'tonic triad' is a triad built on the tonic – scale degree no. 1. The other two notes are scale degrees 3 and 5.

* They stack on top of each other and look sort of like a set of traffic lights! (This is also called 'root position'.)

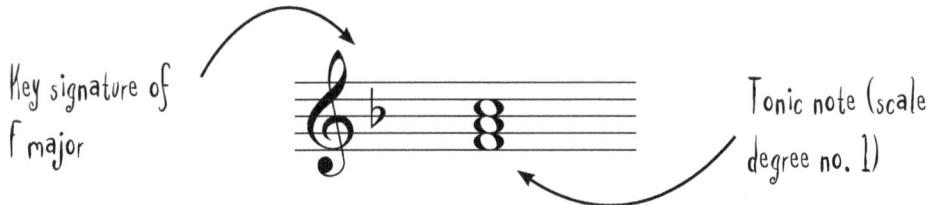

The above chord is the tonic triad of which key? _____

What are the names of the three notes in the triad? _____

Try drawing these tonic triads. Check the clef, and use the correct key signature!

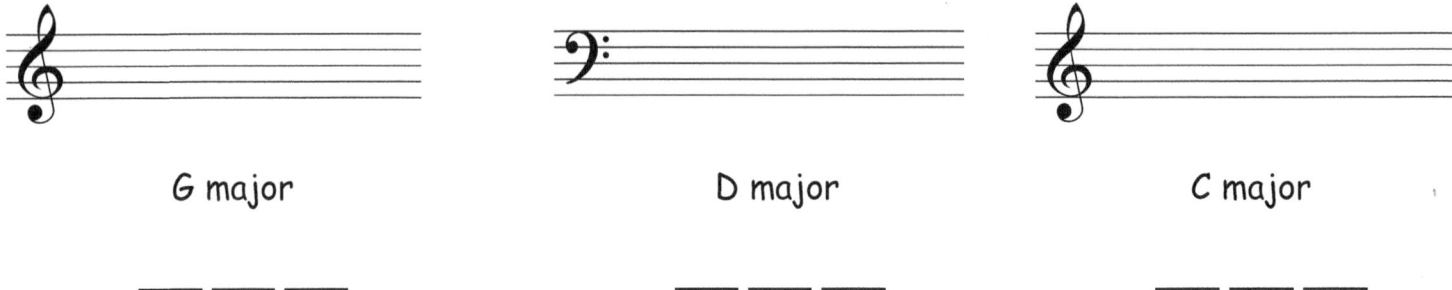

G major   D major   C major

___ ___ ___   ___ ___ ___   ___ ___ ___

Write the letter names underneath the three triads above (be extra careful with the D major chord!).

And now, here are the tonic triads of our four major keys, written with accidentals instead of a key signature.

F major   C major   D major needs an accidental!   G major

Tonic Triad Practice

1. A tonic triad is made up of scale degrees ___, ___ and ___

2. Complete these tonic triads above the given note, then insert the correct key signature (watch out for clef changes):

   C major   G major   G major   D major   F major

3. Write these tonic triads. Use a key signature.

   D major   F major   G major

4. Name the key of these tonic triads, then write the letter names of each.

5. True or false: Hermione Granger and Viktor Krum end up married. _____

6. Which three notes make up a C major triad? _____

Revision of Things

1. Name these tonic triads.

   _____   _____   _____

2. How many semiquavers are there in three minims? _____

3. Just for fun, name this note:    _____

4. At each place marked with a *, write the correct scale degree (e.g. 1st, 2nd etc.).

5. Now rewrite the above melody with correct grouping and beaming of the notes. Draw the clef, key signature and time signature.

6. In the melody you just wrote, find and circle three consecutive notes that make up the tonic triad of F major.

7. Name these harmonic intervals. In what key are they? _____

   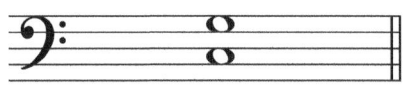   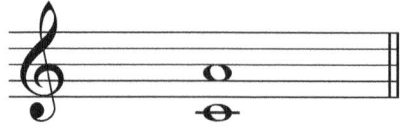   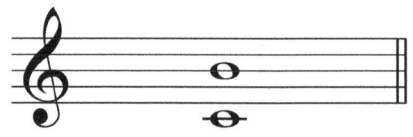

   _____   _____   _____

Word Search

This word search is different from most... the words hidden in the grid are actually the answers to the clues at the bottom of the page!

```
N I T S L O W E R S E T
O U L E N E D L D S R O
S E A E L E I P P I H N
I L E A G O G U A G W I
N L A S C E W D S H L C
U G N T G L R E O E R N
L A A L N I C L S H L P
N V C N I E E P I T R I
E O R S S B D M H N K A
E R U T A N G I S Y E K
L V S R R O R S C E I S
V I I U H D P C I C W L
M O S F P M I N I M A C
```

1. Which goes first after the clef: key signature or time signature?
2. Formal name for the time signature of two crotchet beats per bar.
3. On which line of the staff does the minim rest sit? Third/fourth/fifth?
4. Another name for the 'semibreve' rest is the _____ ___ rest.
5. The only Zodiac sign with three letters. (This probably won't be tested in the Grade 1 theory exam)
6. Technical name for scale degree no. 1.
7. Proper name for distance of an 8th.
8. When marking semitones in a scale, which note do we start from, lowest or highest?
9. Number of tones in a major scale.
10. Short lines used for notes above or below the staff.
11. An interval where both notes are exactly the same pitch.
12. 'Rall.' means to become gradually _____ . (See next page!)
13. You won't find a _____ rest in simple duple or simple triple time.
14. Collective name for sharps, flats and naturals.
15. Chord consisting of three notes.

Terms and Signs

This page lists all the Italian terms you need to know for your exam, and the next page shows all the signs. You have probably already come across many of these in your pieces. You can also download this list from **www.blitzbooks.com**, and it's a great idea to check out **How To Blitz Musical Knowledge!**

Adagio	-	slowly
Andante	-	at an easy walking pace
Moderato	-	at a moderate speed
Allegro	-	lively and fast
Accelerando (accel.)	-	gradually becoming faster
Allegretto	-	moderately fast
Rallentando (rall.)	-	gradually becoming slower
Ritardando (rit. / ritard.)	-	gradually becoming slower
Ritenuto (riten. / rit.)	-	immediately slower
A tempo	-	return to former speed ('in time')
Cantabile	-	in a singing style
Da Capo al fine (D.C. al fine)	-	from the beginning until the word 'fine'
Dal Segno (D.S.) 𝄋	-	from the sign
Leggiero	-	lightly
Molto	-	very
Poco	-	a little
Crescendo (cresc.)	-	gradually becoming louder
Decrescendo (decresc.)	-	gradually becoming softer
Diminuendo (dim.)	-	gradually becoming softer
Lento	-	slowly
Legato	-	smooth, well connected
Staccato	-	short and detached
M.M. ♩=80	-	Maelzel's metronome, 80 beats per minute

Sign	Name	Meaning
⟨	crescendo	gradually becoming louder
⟩	decrescendo/diminuendo	gradually becoming softer
♩.	staccato	short and detached
mf, f, ff	mezzo-forte, forte, fortissimo	moderately loud, loud, very loud ('m' and 'f' always written lower case)
mp, p, pp	mezzo-piano, piano, pianissimo	moderately soft, soft, very soft ('m' and 'p' always written lower case)
(slur notation)	slur	play smoothly (can be over two or more notes)
(tie notation)	tie	play the first note and hold for value of both
𝄐	pause or 'fermata'	hold for longer than written value
>	accent	play strongly
𝄆 𝄇	repeat	repeat the music between the dots
8va------- or 8vb-------	'ottava' sign (over or under notes)	play one octave higher or lower than written

And now, just for fun... to the melody below, add **staccato** signs to the rest of the **crotchets** (notice how the dot goes in the space nearest the note head), add a **tie** (there's only one place it could go), add a **pause** to the last note, and add a sign that says to play the third bar **one octave higher**!

Know Your Signs

Study the melody below and then answer these questions:

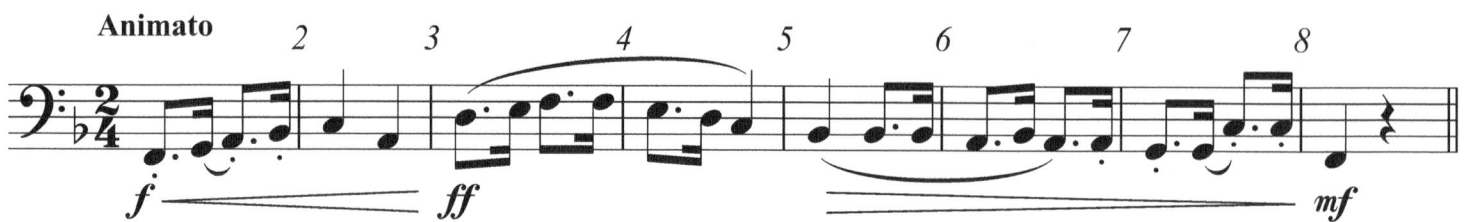

a) What is the loudest dynamic in the melody? _____ Which bar is it? _____

b) Which bars do NOT have this rhythm: ♪♩ _____

c) How many notes are marked staccato? _____ How should these be played? _____

d) Write an Italian word above the first bar that means 'to play lively and fast'.

e) Add a sign to show that the melody should be repeated.

f) Add a pause sign to the highest note.

Here is another melody, by the composer Antonín Dvořák. Answer the following questions:

a) What does '*p*' stand for and what does it mean? _____

b) In which bar does the melody get louder? _____

c) What is the value of each rest in bar 2? _____

d) Add a sign to show that bar 2 should be played one octave higher.

e) How many beats does the longest slur contain? (bars 4-5) _____

f) What does the bottom '4' in the time signature mean? _____

Timed Test II

Once again, time yourself doing this quiz. Do it as fast as you can, then record your finishing time above. But remember, your teacher will **ADD ON 10 SECONDS** for every mistake you make! It's fun to go fast, but more important to be **accurate**. Good luck!

1. Name two Italian terms that mean 'gradually becoming softer':

   _____ and _____

2. What does 'legato' mean? _____

3. Add the correct time signature to this melody:

___   ___   ___   ___   ___

4. Now write the correct scale-degree numbers under the first note of each bar!

5. Why did the chicken cross the road? (OK you don't really have to answer this) _____

6. Fill in this grid:

Sign	Name of Sign	Meaning of Sign
(fermata)		
(crescendo)		
(sixteenth rest)		

STOP THE CLOCK – FILL IN YOUR TIME AT THE TOP!

☐ I made no mistakes!
I keep my time of _____ !

☐ I made _____ mistakes.
My new time is _____ .

53

Copying Music

One of the things you have to do in the exam is show off your fabulously neat music handwriting, and your skills of observation. You have to copy out **some** or **all** of a given melody (read the question carefully) and it has to contain EXACTLY the same details.

Here is a rather well-known nursery rhyme melody, with lots of added terms and signs.

Here is an example of a copying attempt that would not get very high marks.

As you can see, it's important to include EVERYTHING! Right... your turn now... copy the melody above, including all of the details like dynamics and tempo markings!

Here is another melody, 'Ave Maria' by Schubert. Copy bar **1 to the end of bar 3** with ALL the details. The only thing you don't have to include in your answer is the bar numbers.

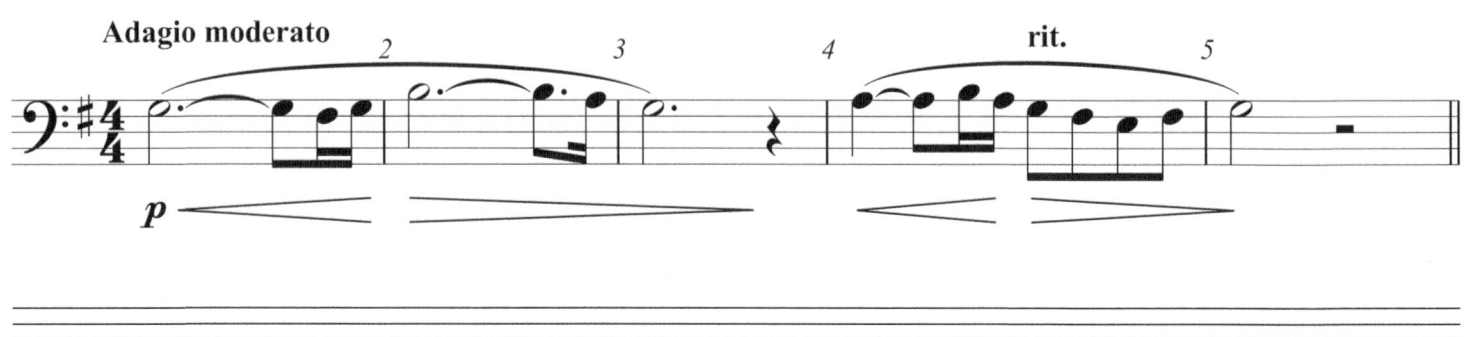

In the exam, you always have to answer some questions about the music before you copy it out. Here's a melody based on a theme by Mendelssohn:

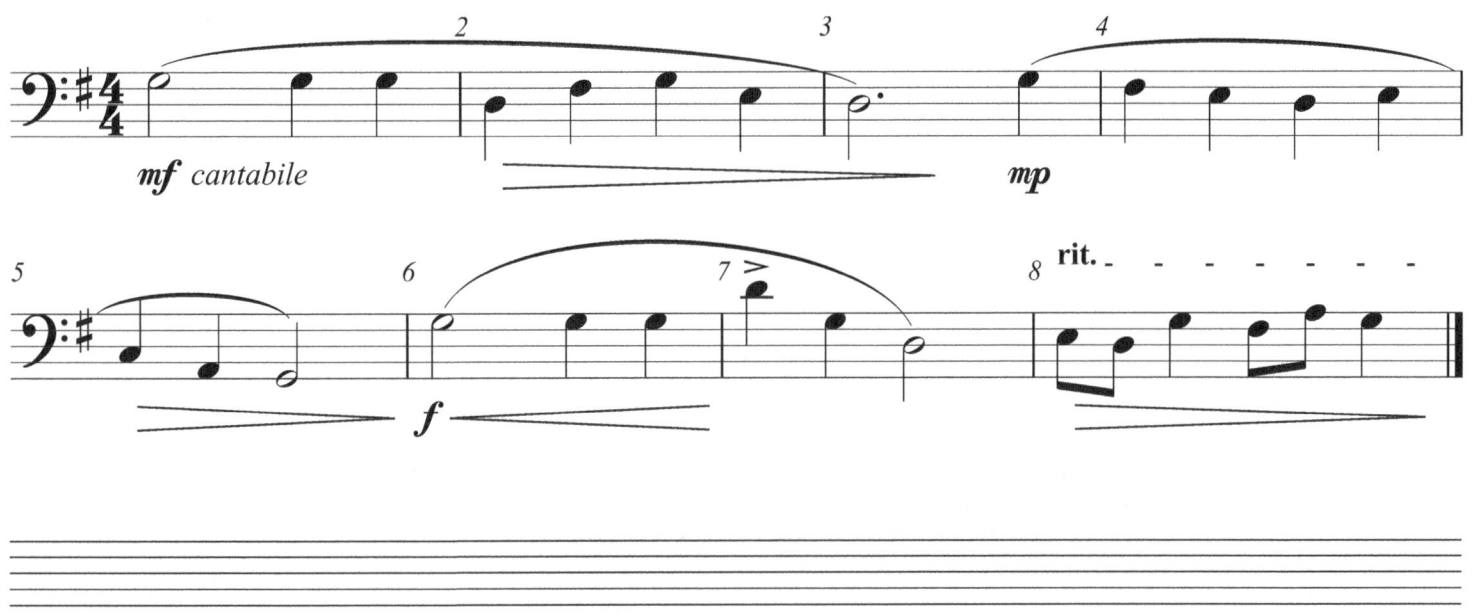

(a) Give the meaning of each of these:

i. *cantabile* _____

ii. **mp** _____

iii. > (bar 7) _____

iv. **f** _____

v. **rit.** (bar 8) _____

(b) Some more questions...

i. What does the time signature mean? _____

ii. Draw a circle around the lowest note.

iii. How many times does a 'diminuendo' sign appear? _____

iv. Give the time name (e.g. crotchet) of the shortest note: _____

v. What colour is C3PO from *Star Wars*? _____ (not essential Grade 1 knowledge)

(c) Copy out the music from the start of the melody **to the end of bar 4** (did you read that last bit carefully?), exactly as it is written above. Don't forget the clef, key signature, time signature, tempo marking, dynamics and all other details. Write the music on the blank stave above question (a). (This is pretty much exactly how you're asked to do it in the exam!)

55

The Very Last Revision Test (promise)

1. Study this melody by Wagner and then answer the questions below.

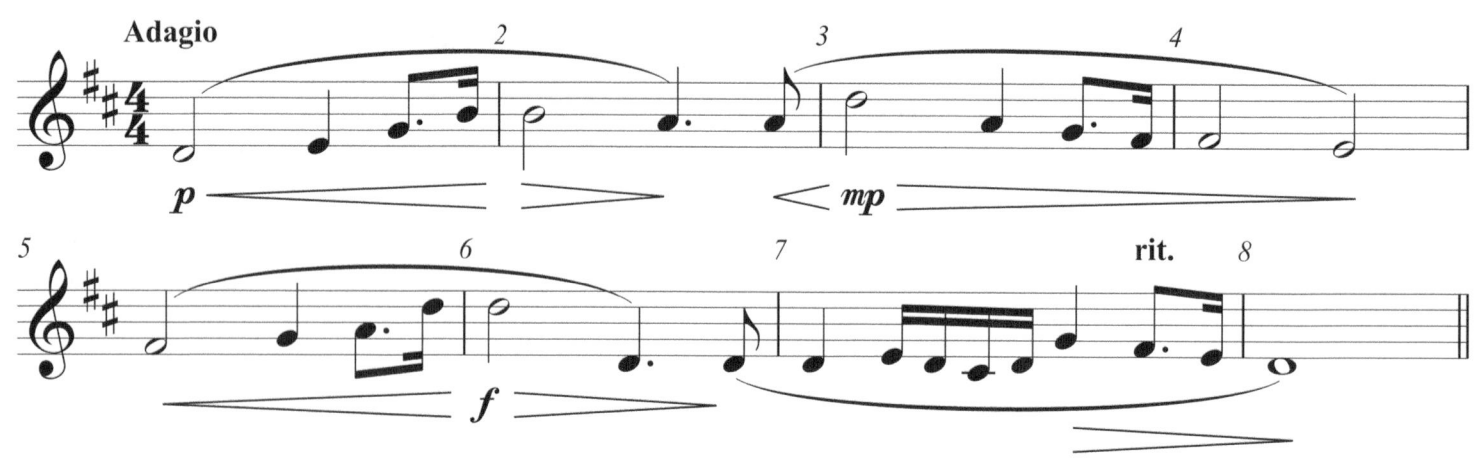

a) What does 'Adagio' mean? _____

b) What is the loudest dynamic marking in the melody? _____

c) What does 'rit.' mean? (end of bar 7) _____

d) What key is this piece in? _____

e) How many times does the rhythm 'dotted quaver semiquaver' appear? _____

f) What colour is a purple finch? (Hint: it's not what you think) _____

g) Give the time name (e.g. crotchet) of the longest note: _____

h) Copy out the music from the **start of bar 5 to the end of bar 8,** exactly as it is written above, including every tiny detail!

2. Rewrite these notes/rests in order from longest to shortest:

3. Write the correct scale degree at each place marked with an asterisk. You'll need to work out the key of the melody to know which note is the '1st' scale degree.

4. Add the missing time signature, then name the key.

Key: _____

5. Add the missing rest or rests.

6. Write these tonic triads with their key signatures. Check the clef.

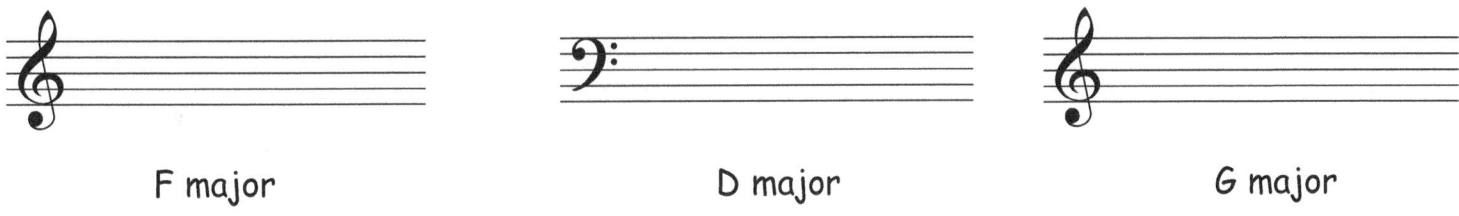

F major   D major   G major

fabulous work!

Mad Multiple Choice

1. Legato means:
   A. smooth and detached
   B. short and well connected
   C. smooth and well connected

2. This note  is:
   A. E sharp
   B. E
   C. E natural

3. Accidentals go:
   A. on the left (before)
   B. on the right (after)
   C. underneath

4. Circle the best treble clef:

5. G major has:
   A. a B flat
   B. four sharps
   C. an F sharp

6. Major scales follow this pattern:
   A. TTSSTTSS
   B. TTSTTTS
   C. TSTSTSTS

7. Circle the correct way to draw a harmonic 3rd above F: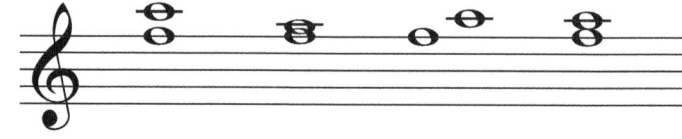

8. Name this interval:  A. 17th

   B. 1st

   C. 8ve

9. When writing scale-degree numbers under melodies:

   A. we use numbers 1-7

   B. we use the numbers 1st-7th

   C. A or B

10. Name this sign:  A. Slur

    B. Tie

    C. Staccato

11. Circle the correct way to draw a B flat:

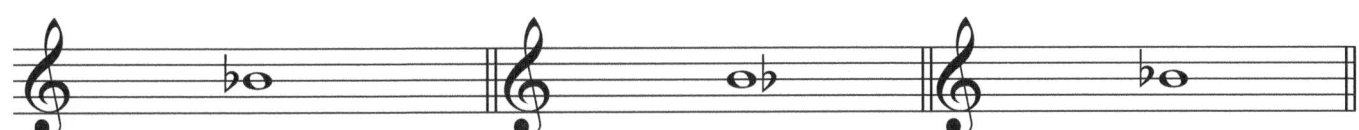

12. Quavers should be grouped: A.   in twos or fours

    B.   in eights or twos

    C.   in threes or fours

13. We should learn our Italian terms because:

    A.   the teacher told us to

    B.   we should understand what they mean in the music we play

    C.   we might visit Italy one day

14. Circle the most accurate way to write a 7th above G: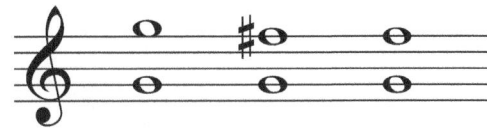

59

15. What's wrong with this leger line note?

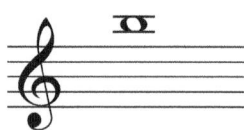

    A.   The top leger line is unnecessary
    B.   The circle is too small
    C.   Nothing, it's perfect

16. The sign  means:
    A.   crescendo
    B.   gradually becoming softer
    C.   all of the above

17. Allegro means:
    A.   fast and lively
    B.   very fast
    C.   extremely fast

18. A double bar-line  means:
    A.   the end of a piece
    B.   the beginning of a piece
    C.   the end of a piece or important section

19. You should not use minim rests in:
    A.   Simple duple time
    B.   Simple quadruple time
    C.   Simple triple time

(Hint: There are two correct answers to question 19!)

20. Middle C lives:
    A.   above the bass staff
    B.   below the treble staff
    C.   A and B

Test Paper... sort of

All theory books end with a test paper, but this one is DIFFERENT. It already has the answers in it (mostly wrong answers!) and your job is to be the teacher – you have to **mark** it.

When you've found all the mistakes, go to **www.blitzbooks.com** and download the EXACT SAME PAPER – this time with no answers already in it. See if you can get 100%!

Theory Paper Grade 1

Time Allowed: 1.5 hours

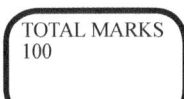

1\. Add the missing bar-lines to these two tunes. The first bar-line is given.

In what key are both the melodies above? __C major and A minor__

2\. a) Draw a circle around the *lower* note of each of these pairs of notes.

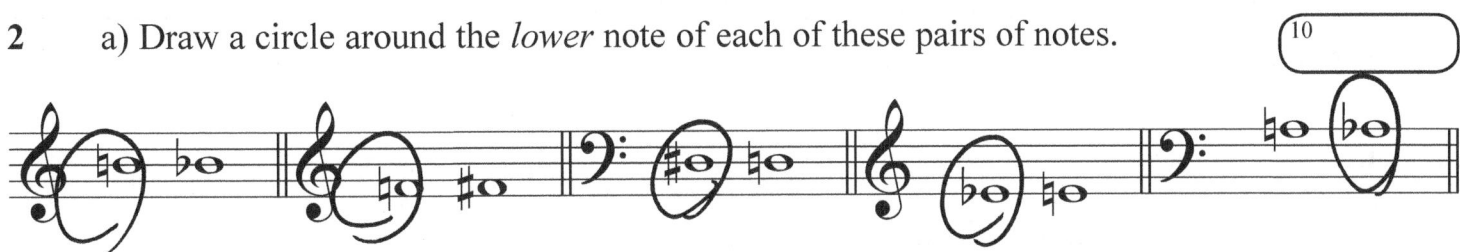

b) Draw a circle around the *higher* note of each of these pairs of notes.

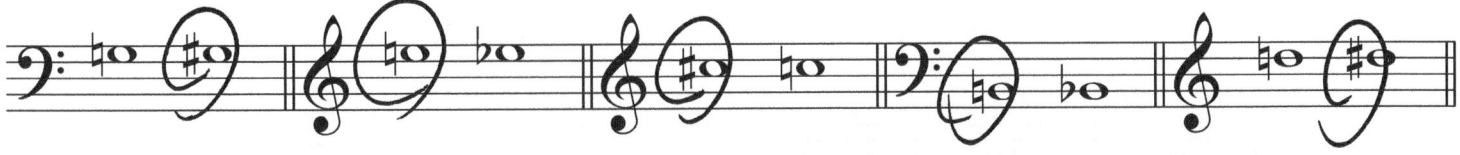

3   In each of the following melodies, add a rest at each place marked with an asterisk to make the bar complete.

4   Give the letter name of each of the notes marked *, including the flat sign where necessary.

5   Write as semibreves (whole notes) the scales named below.

Do *not* use a key signature, but remember to add any necessary accidentals.

D major, ascending

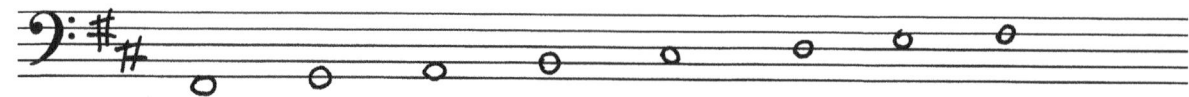

F major, descending

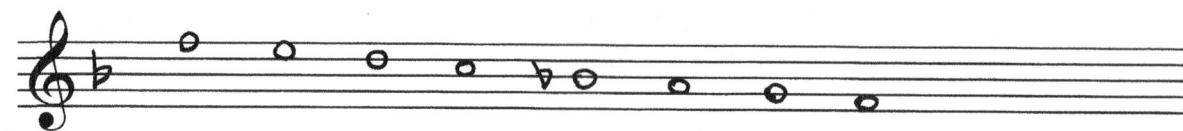

6 Give the number (e.g. 5th, 7th) of each of these melodic intervals. The key is G major.

3rd   4th   7th

7th   8

7 Write the equivalent rest for each of these notes.

8 Tick one box for each term/sign, as shown in the first answer.

𝄐 means:

- accent the note ☐
- staccato; detached ☐
- pause on the note ✓
- play the note with mute ☐

(two notes with slur) means:

- slur; perform smoothly ✓
- slur; detached ☐
- tie; detached ☐
- tie; hold for the value of both notes ☐

Leggiero means:

- in a singing style ☐
- lightly ✓
- smoothly ☐
- slowly ☐

8va⁻⁻⁻⁻⁻⁻ means:

- play one octave lower ☐
- play one octave higher ☐
- play also the octave above ✓
- play the note with mute ☐

(crescendo) means:

- accent the note ☐
- loud ☐
- gradually getting louder ✓
- gradually getting quieter ☐

♩. means:

- play detached ✓
- accent the note ☐
- play loudly ☐
- hold for longer than the written value ☐

9 Look at this melody by Georges Bizet and then answer the questions below.

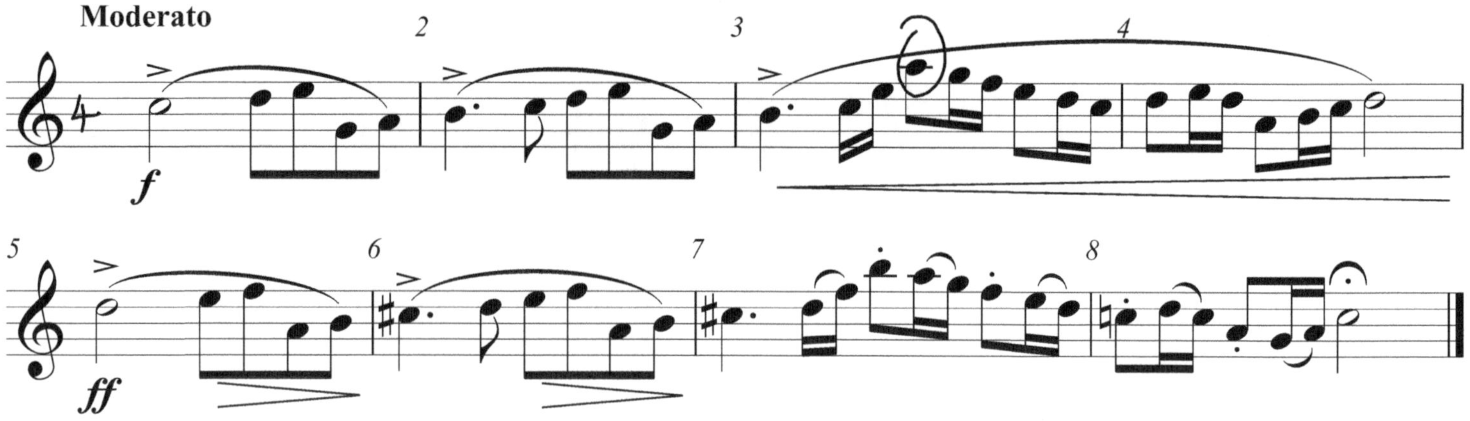

[Musical score: Moderato, 8 bars, with student's handwritten copy on blank stave below labeled "F" and "get louder here"]

(a) Give the English meaning of each of these:

i. *ff* — super forte

ii. 𝄐 (e.g. bar 8) — pause the game or piece

iii. > (e.g. first note) — mini diminuendo

iv. **Moderato** — at a moderate speed

v. ♩̇ — staccato = spikey

(b) Complete the following:

i. Add the correct time signature at the beginning.

ii. How many bars do NOT have accents? 3

iii. Draw a circle around the highest note.

iv. From what number platform does the Hogwarts Express leave? 9¾ ha ha ha

v. In which bars is the player told to increase volume? 3, 4, 5, 6

(c) Copy out the music from the start of the melody to the end of bar 4, exactly as it is written above. Don't forget the clef, key signature, time signature, tempo marking, dynamics and all other details. Write the music on the blank stave above question (a).
(Marks will be given for neatness and accuracy.)